REFLECTIONS OF TASAWWUF

*Essays, Poems, and Narrative*
*on Sufi Themes*

BY THE SAME AUTHOR

*Doorkeeper of the Heart: Versions of Rabi'a*

*Hammering Hot Iron:*
*A Spiritual Critique of Robert Bly's* Iron John

*The System of Antichrist:*
*Truth and Falsehood in Postmodernism and the New Age*

*Cracks in the Great Wall:*
*The UFO Phenomenon and Traditional Metaphysics*

*Legends of the End:*
*Prophecies of the End Times, Antichrist,*
*Apocalypse, and Messiah from Eight Religious Traditions*

*The Virtues of the Prophet:*
*A Young Muslim's Guide to the Greater Jihad,*
*The War Against the Passions*

*Knowings: In the Arts*
*of Metaphysics, Cosmology, and the Spiritual Path*

*Who is the Earth?*
*How To See God in the Natural World*

*Folk Metaphysics:*
*Mystical Meanings in Traditional Folk Songs and Spirituals*

*Shadow of the Rose:*
*The Esoterism of the Romantic Tradition*
(with Jennifer Doane Upton)

*The Wars of Love*

CHARLES UPTON

# Reflections
## of
## *Tasawwuf*

*Essays, Poems, and Narrative
on Sufi Themes*

SOPHIA PERENNIS

SAN RAFAEL, CA

First published in the USA
by Sophia Perennis
© Charles Upton 2008

Series editor: James R. Wetmore

For information, address:
Sophia Perennis, P.O. Box 151011
San Rafael, CA 94915
sophiaperennis.com

Library of Congress Cataloging-in-Publication Data

Upton, Charles, 1948–
Reflections of tasawwuf: essays, poems and narrative
on Sufi themes / by Charles Upton.

p. cm.
ISBN 978-1-59731-078-9 (pbk: alk. paper)
1. Sufism. 2. Sufism—Doctrines. I. Title.
BP189.U726 2008
297.4—dc22                2008003158

# CONTENTS

# PREFACE

IN THE WORDS OF Abu Bakr Siraj al-Din (Martin Lings), 'Sufism is central, exalted, profound and mysterious; it is inexorable, exacting, powerful, dangerous, aloof — and necessary.' It is by this very exaltation and aloofness that, like a watchtower set on a mountain, the light of *Tasawwuf* reaches far. What Sufism is in itself can only be lived, but the reflections of its light off any polished surface within its range — philosophy, theology, poetry, narrative, fable, science, mathematics, psychology, alchemy — actually can be put into words; accurate words; words capable of returning an infinitesimal fraction of the light they echo to the Source that sent it. (The true return, the full restitution, is in the darkness of God Alone.) This is why I have titled this book *Reflections of* (not *on*) *Tasawwuf*. If you set a mirror facing directly toward the Sun, the ray of Return is swallowed up in the ray of Revelation. But if you turn the mirror so that its ray falls on this or that object of the world, then those who are not standing in direct sunlight, like the inhabitants of Plato's Cave who can't yet stand the fullness of the light, will at least know the position of the Sun. The itinerary does not accomplish the journey, but it is a necessary aspect of the preliminary orientation.

The reflected light of the Sun is a pale golden yellow. The unmediated light of the Sun, to those staring directly at its disk, is blue-black, the color of the midnight sky. Perhaps the stars, that appear white to us, are actually black; perhaps the midnight sky, that appears black to our eyes, is in reality the very face of the Sun.

If there were a dark night
In which darkness itself was visible,
What eye could see it?
If the Sun stepped out
Through night's curtains at midnight,
Then even before dawn
Night would be at an end
And dawn without a gate.
This is why, in His mercy
God gave the Moon to Muhammad
As a law, a veil, and a warning.

[*after Hafiz*]

# INTRODUCTION

## An Outline of Sufism

WHAT CAN BE SAID about Sufism? Jalaluddin Rumi said, 'there is no such thing as a Sufi in this world—and if there were, he would be non-existent.'

Sufism—*tasawwuf* in Arabic—is Islamic mysticism. Though the Sufis have produced a vast literature of exquisite spiritual poetry— Hafiz, Rumi, and a thousand others—and masterpieces of metaphysics, such as those wrought by Ibn al-'Arabi, the Shaykh al-Akbar, the 'greatest teacher', who was also a great poet—there is nothing essential in Sufism that is not ultimately a commentary on the Holy Qur'an. Those so-called Sufis who try to separate Sufism from Islam are like cut flowers in a vase. Until the water that sustains them evaporates, they bloom and give off fragrance—but in reality they possess only the semblance of life, and the power to reproduce is forever denied them. Though he was not called by that name, the Prophet Muhammad, peace and blessings be upon him, was really the first Sufi. And the most widely acknowledged prototype and exemplar of Sufism, chosen recipient of the Prophet's inner teachings, was the fourth Sunni caliph and the first Shi'ite Imam, the Prophet's son-in-law Ali ibn Abi Talib, peace and blessings be upon him.

In the first generation or two after the Prophet's death, the Sufis had no name of their own, but after the current of history began to sweep Islam further away from the purity of its origins, the early Muslim ascetics were transformed into the Sufis, and Sufi 'orders' began to be established around great saints and teachers, to concentrate the inner teachings and the spiritual practices of Islam. A Sufi order is roughly analogous to a Catholic monastic order, except for the fact that the normal practice of Sufis is to meet in 'lodges' known as *zawiyas* (Arabic) or *khaniqas* (Persian) or *tekkes* (Turkish).

Generally speaking, Sufis are not cloistered like monks (in the words of the Prophet, peace and blessings be upon him, 'there is no monasticism in Islam') and are usually married (in the words of the Prophet, 'marriage is half the religion'). And also unlike Catholic monastic orders, Sufi orders are independent; they are 'chartered' by no authority outside their own masters and lineages, though traditional Sufi orders nonetheless live by generally accepted Muslim norms. Sufism as a whole is not a sect as are Sunni and Shi'ite Islam; Sufi orders, though they are (at least nominally) either Sunni or Shi'ite, are institutions unto themselves. Sufism thus represents a kind of independent, though not separate, 'estate' within Islam: that of the 'organized mystics'.

The word 'Sufi' is derived from the Arabic word for 'wool' (root *swf*) from which the rough garments of the of the poor were made—or from the word for 'purity' (*safa*)—or from the Greek word for wisdom (*sophia*). A Sufi is commonly known in Arabic as a *faqir*—'poor man'—or, in Persian, a *darvish,* which means the same thing, with the connotation of 'thresholder', in the sense of a beggar hanging on the doorsill, hoping for a handout. A Sufi is poor in the sense of Jesus' words when He said, 'blessed are the poor in spirit, for they shall see God.' A Sufi is a poor man because he recognizes his own intrinsic poverty, which is the intrinsic poverty of all things other than God. According to Sufi doctrine, only God possesses being in His own right; all other things possess it only as a gift of That One. In themselves, they are nothing.

The essential practice of Sufism is to remember God and forget oneself. The essential form this practice takes, beyond the practices common to all Muslims (such as the daily prayer) is known as *dhikr,* 'remembrance'. *Dhikr* or *zekr* is the occasional group vocal recitation, and the constant, individual, silent recitation, of God's name, or a formula containing it, or another Name referring to a particular aspect of God. Various forms of meditation and spiritual retreat are also practiced. Music, poetry and dance are sometimes also used as collateral supports. These practices differ from order to order, with the *dhikr*, however, being effectively universal.

The Sufi's Master is, to him, the very presence of God. He can be this for his followers not because he has become Godlike in his human nature, but because he has become nothing. He is an open door through which streams the Divine Light. One Sufi master has said: 'If the master is not perfect, the darvish will worship him, and to worship one's master is the same as worshipping oneself.' It is the Master who admits the prospective darvish to his order and his presence, gives him (God willing) both the right and the power to invoke the Name of God, and transmits to him the *baraka* (grace) of his spiritual lineage (*silsilah*), which stretches back usually to Ali ibn Abi Talib but sometimes to the first Sunni Caliph, Abu Bakr, and from there to the Prophet, and from the Prophet to the Angel Gabriel who revealed the Qur'an, and from Gabriel to Allah, the Absolute Reality.

Sufism has a vast metaphysical literature, embodying a complex and sophisticated understanding of the ways and planes and dimensions of being through which the Absolute Reality of Allah manifests itself, and an equally vast literature on spiritual psychology and the various 'states' and 'stations' through which the Sufi passes on his path to God—or, rather, his path *in* God. States are gifts of God which can be neither merited nor produced at will; 'stations' are spiritual achievements of the Sufi himself, based upon his ability to actualize the virtues—virtues like humility, zeal, trust in God, etc. States may announce stations; they may even be considered virtual stations in themselves; but only the labor to necessary assimilate the freely-bestowed grace of a state can turn it into a station. God may plant the grain, water it, harvest it, thresh it, winnow it, grind it, bake it into bread, slice and serve it; He may even place it in our mouths. But it is up to us to chew, swallow and digest it.

Sufi ontology (the science of the nature of being) takes many forms. Ibn al-'Arabi speaks of the Five Hadarat (presences of God): the 'human domain' (*nasut*) or corporeal world; the 'domain or royalty' or angelic world (*malakut*) which has direct sovereignty over the *nasut*; the 'domain of power' (*jabarut*), the celestial or archangelic world; the 'domain of the Divine' (*Lahut*), the realm of the Logos or the Personal God; and the *Hahut*, the domain of the Divine Essence, the Formless Absolute. From another point of view, the world of events (inner and outer) can be seen as the ensemble of God's acts, the world of intelligible realities as his Names or Attributes, and Allah

Himself as a perfect synthesis of those Names. Beyond this lies only the Absolute Essence, which cannot be conceived of and should not even be contemplated. Yet, in a way, the Essence can be known — though not by us. God's Essence can be known only by God; when we are annihilated in our limited selfhoods, then God knows Himself in us. As Abu Bakr said, 'To know that God cannot be known is to know God.'

The complement to Sufi ontology is its anthropology, which deals with the inner structure, or potential development, of the human person. This anthropology takes many forms; perhaps the simplest hierarchical scheme would be the following: first material nature, which today we would call a person's genetic inheritance; then *nafs*, 'soul', most usually in the sense of unconscious ego; next *Qalb* or Heart, the essence of the human being (though not everybody realizes this essence), which may also be seen as the point of established conscious attention, both intrinsic and intentional, the central point of the psyche where it is intersected by the ray of the Spirit, and which has certain affinities with Jung's 'Self Archetype'; then *Ruh*, the Spirit itself, the overflow of God's life and love and knowledge which creates us, and recreates us, in each separate instant of spiritual time (*waqt*); then the inner consciousness (*Sirr* 'Secret') which is deeper than the Spirit, and may have some affinity with the Vedantic *Atman* or indwelling Absolute Witness; and finally the innermost consciousness (*Sirr al-Sirr*, 'the Secret of the Secret'), which is known to God alone and *is* God alone; *Sirr al-Sirr* is perhaps equivalent to the Vedantic *Brahman*, the Absolute in Itself.

In the course of the spiritual Path, the *nafs* is purified and refined. It first appears as 'the commanding *nafs*', the lower passional soul which rules us on the basis of our own whims, desires and self-will, until we submit to God's rule instead and become true *Muslims*. Next appears 'the accusing *nafs*', the troubled conscience, which recognizes the evil of the commanding *nafs*, struggles against it but is ultimately powerless to overcome it. This is followed by 'the inspired *nafs*', which begins to have intimations of higher realities and is able to know and follow what is good for it. And the final development is the '*nafs*-at-peace', the individual self in perfect submission to the Will of God. Some identify the *nafs*-at-peace with the

Heart; at any rate, it opens onto the Heart, which is only firmly established as Heart when the Spirit has finally conquered the *nafs* and subdued it—when the *pneumatic* humanity gains power over and subdues the *psychic* humanity. The witness of this conquest is the *Sirr*; the ultimate Reality beyond all witnessing is the *Sirr al-Sirr*.

The two final stations of the Spiritual Path are *fana*—annihilation (as a separate selfhood) and *baqa*, subsistence in God. Our goal is to become nothing—as the moth consumed by the candle has become annihilated in the light and flame to which it was attracted, as the lover in the act of love is lost and annihilated in his Beloved. And if, after that, we still subsist, it is by God's Will and Grace alone—as indeed it always was. The *nafs* believes it is self-created, or at least acts as if it does; when the *nafs* is ultimately subdued and annihilated, then if we exist, we exist not as we think or believe or fantasize or fear or desire ourselves to be, but as God knows us to be. Who He *knows* us to be is who we really are, from pre-eternity to post-eternity; who we *think* we are has never existed, and never will.

The Prophet Muhammad, peace and blessings be upon him, said: 'Die before you are made to die.' This is the real essence of Sufism, its whole practice, and its final end.

# I

## PRACTICE

What does the Beloved's beauty
Need with our own flawed beauty?
Loveliness Itself requires neither makeup, nor
    rouge,
Nor painted mole, nor pencilled eyebrow.

When I saw that every day Joseph became more
    beautiful,
I knew that love for him would bring out Zulaikha
From behind the curtain of virginity.

*[after Hafiz]*

# DIMENSIONS OF *NAMAZ*

*Namaz* is the word used for the Muslim daily prayer in the Persian and Turkish languages, the equivalent of the Arabic *salat*. The following esoteric exegesis of the daily prayer is based on the form used by a traditional Persian sufi order, which incorporates not only the first *surah* of the Qur'an — *al-Fatihat* or 'The Opening' — as virtually all Muslim prayer-forms do, but also the one-hundred twelfth *surah*, *at-Tauhid* or 'The Unity'. 'The Opening' lies under the sign of *tashbih*, the Divine Immanence, the 'comparability' of God, and 'The Unity' under that of *tanzih*, the 'incomparability' of God, the Divine Transcendence.

The five daily prayers are the visible essence of Muslim spirituality, just as submission to the will of God, with every breath, is the invisible essence. *Namaz* is called 'obligatory' because is derives from Necessary Being; it is an expression of the immutable truth of the human form in relation to its Absolute Source. We are required to pray because we are required to be what we are — to fully actualize the potential of the human state.

*Namaz* is a cycle of symbolic actions, dense with meaning, which reenact the entire manifestation and reintegration of the universe, and contain the total form of the spiritual path. When we pray the daily prayer, the universe and the Lord of the universe are polarized and united in a single gesture. And the reality which unfolds manifest existence from its Source and reintegrates it into its Source is the essence of the human form itself.

The prerequisite for annihilation is polarity; the first step in self-effacement is for the self to stand forth clearly enough to be effaced. If God is to be anything more than a dream dreamt by the self while lost to itself in dreams, the self must wake up, and meet god 'face to Face'. 'He who knows himself knows his Lord' [prophetic *hadith*] because he who awakens to himself, and remembers himself, thereby encounters his Lord. The daily prayer — which, according to

Ibn al-'Arabi, 'can correctly be divided between the servant and God' [William Chittick, *The Sufi Path of Knowledge*, 1989, p 327] — is the essence of this encounter (as, on another level, is the encounter between the disciple and the spiritual Master).

The human being is both *'abd* — the powerless slave of God — and *khalifa* — the fully-empowered representative of God. When we humble ourselves, we receive the Divine Command, and carry it into manifestation. When we are annihilated, then nothing but That One remains in the locus of our form. We die as self-defined identity and are simultaneously reborn as *symbol:* if only God is, and yet we still appear, what else could we conceivably be? In prayer, we are not our desires, our fears, our virtues, our sins, or our personal history: we are Humanity as such.

❖

There is no end to the layers of meaning surrounding the essence of *namaz*; all I can do here is arbitrarily choose a few facets of the subject, and suggest something of their depth.

*Bismillah er-Rahman er-Rahim* — the '*basmala*' which opens all surahs of the Qur'an but one—contains the whole relationship between God as Cosmic Manifestation and God as Source and Essence. As such it represents the Divine Reality which encompasses and resolves the polarity *God/Cosmos*; this is why it is the quintessential verse of blessing in the religion of Islam.

Given that Mercy is intimacy with God and Wrath is distance from Him, *Rahman* is Mercy ultimately resulting in Wrath, while *Rahim* is the face of Wrath opening into Mercy. *Rahman* creates the universe; *Rahim* returns universal manifestation to its invisible Source. *Rahman* is the root of what Ibn al-'Arabi calls God's *Will*, the principle of all that actually is and occurs, whether good or evil. *Rahman* is the Mercy that allows all things to be what they are—and one of the consequences of this Mercy is that all things are free to depart from their Divine Source, to flee their Center, to enter a world of partiality and fragmentation, where the possibilities known as evil, suffering and ignorance become actualized. Potential existence cries out to be created and individuated, and *Rahman*,

God's universal Mercy, answers 'Yes'. But created, individuated existence also cries out, begging to be freed from the chains of contingency, just as potential existence begged to be freed from the bonds of nonentity. The divine 'Yes' to this second cry is God's particular Mercy, *Rahim*, identified by Ibn al-'Arabi with God's *Wish*, His desire that all things be saved, return to Him and experience His Goodness. So, in the most universal sense, all pleas are granted, none are denied; this is what Ibn al-'Arabi means when he says that 'the determined determines the Determiner.' God, the Only Being, since He can never be other than Himself, can therefore deny Himself nothing. And there is a moment, the moment when all possible existences are still hidden within the Divine Nature, but poised on the brink of manifestation, when they peer into the shining bubble of that manifestation, into the great round of existence, and foresee all possible ignorance, suffering and evil, and see it as God, and know it as good, agree to it all beforehand. This is the pre-eternal covenant [Q. 7:172] in which God asks *Am I not your Lord?*, to which all possible things, trembling on the brink of existence, answer: *Yea!*

*Rahman* is the Mercy that says 'yes' to all things, while *Rahim* is the Mercy that says 'yes' to some things and 'no' to others—the mercy of limitation, of the victory of redeeming form over brutal chaos, of *sirat al-mostaqim*, the Straight Path of return. And the deepest center of *Rahim* is the knowledge that our suffering of the Wrath of God is none other than our resistance to the Mercy of God—that the fire our ego encounters, burning in the dark abyss of God, is, in its own nature, nothing but a cool, fresh-water sea of infinite Mercy. *Rahman* allows Reality to be veiled by its own manifestation, thereby making possible illusion and ignorance; it is the divine creative act that unfolds a universe apparently other than God and claiming itself as a partner to Him, the illusion inherent in the verse [Q. 36:82]: *His command, when he desires a thing, is to say to it 'Be!' and it is*—because how could He speak that word to a thing unless it already existed, in potential, within Him, just as the motion of one's arm is potential to that arm, without thereby being a second entity added to it? *Kun!* ('Be!') does not change the nature or position of any single thing, but merely veils real existence with its manifestation as apparent existence. As the Prophet Muhammad said, peace and blessings be upon him: '[Before creation] Allah was, and there was nothing beside him,' to which Ali ibn Abi Talib answered, 'And He is even now as he was.' And *Rahim*, in one sense, is also illusion—the effective, empowering and saving illusion that, even if God is the only Being, mercifully there is still a way to say 'yes' to some things and 'no' to others. We say 'no' to illusion until we realize that illusion doesn't even exist to say 'no' to. And we say 'yes' to God until we realize that nothing outside God exists. In absolute terms our 'yes' is both impossible and unnecessary, since it is identical with God as Necessary Being, in Whom all possible Being is eternally realized, and Necessary Being is neither established by our 'yes' nor negated by our 'no'. But in terms of the 'saving veil' of *Rahim*, we are allowed, and empowered, to choose That which is beyond all choice. The Absolute does not exclude the relative but embraces it; this is the essence of God's Mercy.

This is a tiny fragment of the significance of the *basmallah*, a single verse of the Muslim daily prayer. It reveals the motion of universal manifestation and the motion of universal return-to-Source as simultaneous, embedded as one in the Divine Nature; as a plucked string vibrating between the two poles of Comparability (*tashbih* or Immanence) and Incomparability (*tanzih* or Transcendence) to produce a single wave or tone which is the name *Allah*; and as the motionless baseline of that wave, in which *Rahman* and *Rahim* are not two complementary motions, but a single Path, *sirat al-mosta-qim*, on which it is known that the first step of departure from God is also the last step of return to Him, and therefore that for His Essence to depart from His Essence is not possible. It never occurred. As the Sufi saying goes, 'In the Night I heard a voice whispering, "There is no such thing as a voice whispering in the Night."' Departing and returning apply only to the kind of 'figurative' being we possess, not to Absolute Being.

❖

The *basmallah* is included in the *fatihah*, the 'opening' of both the *namaz* and the Qur'an, and the *fatihat* is the opening of Being. In the *basmallah* we know God as departing from and returning to

Himself in a single motion, in the secret of His own nature, without literal departure or literal return; the *basmallah*, in this sense, indicates the eternal potential within God for His manifestation of the universe. When we say *Alhamdo-lillahe rabbel-alemin, ar-rahmane-rahim*, we posit the projection of this motionless and eternal resonance within the Divine Nature as the field of universal manifestation, by which God is Lord of the Worlds, the Essence of all possible experiences—an Essence which cannot be experienced in Itself. But as soon as we *identify* with experience, we invoke the end and dissolution of all experience, the Angel of Death. Thus God is not only the Essence of experience but also the End of experience, *Maleke yomeddin*, the King of the Day of Judgment. When we come before this King, as we will when the end of this cycle dawns upon the earth; as we will when we come to die; as we do already, whether we know it or not, between each breath and the next, if we have not died before we are made to die, if we have not realized God as *Rabbel-alemin*, we will experience *yomeddin* as wrath. *Rabbel-alemin* is the Comparability of God, the universe of experience as the symbolic manifestation of That One, the Divine Immanence. *Maleke yomeddin* is the Incomparability of God, the annihilation of both experience and experiencer, the Divine Transcendence. And in Eternity, God as Lord of the Worlds and God as King of the Day of Judgment are simultaneous in subsistence and One in Essence.

*Edenas-seratel mostaqim, seratal-lazina anamta alihem, ghirel maghzube valaz-zallin* (*Show is the straight path, the path of those whom Thou hast favored, not of those who earn Thy anger or those who go astray*, [Q. 1:1–7]) reminds us of the possibility of the encounter with Divine wrath, and that other manifestation of wrath, an endless wandering in hopeless ignorance. It is bracing and saving shock. It is *Rahim*.

The *fatihat* is under the sign of God's Comparability: He is like a Lord of the Worlds; He is like a King sitting in Judgment; He is like a guide on a straight path. But the second part of the *namaz*, the *Sura At-Tauhid*, is under the sign of God's Incomparability. The *fatihat* speaks of manifestation and return, but leaves us dangling with the possibility of endless exile. The *Sura At-Tauhid* speaks of God only as He is in Himself, and so actualizes the return which the *fatihat* only posits. God is One; He is all we need; He proceeds from nothing and generates nothing because there is nothing outside Him; and it is impossible to compare Him with anything because there is nothing other than Him to which He might be compared. The *Sura At-Tauhid* lives on the far side of Judgment, beyond all the worlds.

❖

The prayer positions in *namaz* are also pregnant with symbolism. From the human point of view, the upright position is that of existence, the bowing position that of humility, and the cycle of sitting and prostration that of subsistence and annihilation. Of the prostration, Shaykh Ahmad al-Alawi has written:

> Before his prostration the Gnostic had the upright stature of existence, but after his prostration he hath become extinct, a thing lost, effaced in himself and eternal in his Lord....When the worshipper hath attained the degree of prostration and hath been extinguished from existence, he prostrateth himself a second time that he might be extinguished from that extinction. Thus is his (second) prostration identical with his rising up from the (first) prostration, which rising signifyeth subsistence. [Martin Lings, *A Sufi Saint of the Twentieth Century*, 1973, p. 188]

In line with this view, we could say that the first prostration is annihilation in God; the first rising, subsistence in this world through God (i.e., recognition of our contingency); the second prostration, subsistence in God; and the second rising, annihilation in this world. To the degree that we are annihilated in the Divine Nature, we can—if God wills to return us to existence—know ourselves as presently emanating from, and totally contingent upon, our Lord. And knowing ourselves as totally contingent upon our Lord, we know ourselves as never having been emanated, as never having been created, as unique and particular Names of God, subsisting within God, with no reality but His. And knowing ourselves as never having been created, we know the form of us that remains in this world as no more than a mask, a simulacrum, an empty name. Nor do 'we' ever really know this, only God knows it. (These four knowings are simultaneous, and there is not a hair's-breadth of distinction between them.)

From the Divine point of view, the standing position represents the vertical dimension of Divinity, whereby God is known as hierarchically more exalted and more powerful than any conceivable reality, and the prostration the horizontal dimension, the All-inclusive, the All-encompassing, the Undifferentiated, the Pure. The standing position is thus God in masculine mode, the Divine Act, while the prostration is God in feminine mode, the Divine Substance. The prostration is the pure receptivity of God that is set within us; the standing position is the overwhelming sovereignty of God that is placed above us. While standing, we are God's vice-regent; while prostrate, we are God's slave. (And the reverse is equally true, since when we place ourselves below God hierarchically, we assert our separate existence and so become His slaves, whereas when we are annihilated, we become God's locus-of-manifestation, and that is our delegated sovereignty.) Prostration is the Infinite that gives birth to all forms because it is totally unconditioned by all forms. The upright position is the Absolute which humbles and annihilates all forms because It has absolute precedence over all forms. (And the reverse is equally true: The upright position, insofar as it symbolizes the Hierarchy of Being, represents God's Infinite Self-manifestation, whereas the prostration, insofar as it symbolizes annihilation, represents the truth that, in the face of the Absolute, nothing but the Absolute can claim existence.)

The masculine or standing position is the source of *al-Jalal*, the Majesty of God; the prostration or feminine is the source of *al-Jamal*, the Beauty of God. In *namaz*, we balance *al-Jalal* and *al-Jamal* through the medium of the human body, and unite them; we make a ritual synthesis between the Names of Beauty and the Names of Majesty, and in so doing become the locus-of-manifestation for the Name *Allah*, thus fulfilling the human mandate. *Lo! We offered the Trust unto the heavens and the earth and the hills, but they shrank from bearing it and were afraid of it. And man assumed it.* [Q. 33:72] In a sense we actually become *sirat al-mostaqim*, which on one level is the bridge between this world and the next, the isthmus or *barzakh* between the 'two seas' of material and spiritual existence;

which on a deeper level is the bridge between the Immanence of God and His Transcendence; and which on the deepest level is that bridge between the Infinite and the Absolute which is the Divine Essence itself.

From the point-of-view of manifestation, a bridge unites what is separated. But from the point-of-view of Unity, it separates what is united. Thus Dr. Javad Nurbakhsh, present head of the Nimatullahi Order, has said of *namaz*:

> For the perfect sufi, ritual prayer . . . expresses a state of sobriety, a mood of awareness. It is emergence from the state of unity into the state of sober consciousness. The perfect sufi should spend the rest of his time in a state of unity (*vahdat*). Prayer for the perfect sufi is a descent from the state of unity into a state of worldly awareness, whereas ordinary people make prayer a vehicle to travel towards God. . . . Prayer for the perfect sufi is thus a kind of re-entry into the world of multiplicity. One's balance might become upset if one were to remain in a state of unity, and this balance should be preserved.

❖

In contrast to the position of some sufis, Ibn al-'Arabi teaches that the obligatory works of Islam, including the *namaz*, are higher than the supererogatory works. He identifies the supererogatory works with the Divine Names, and the obligatory works with the Essence. In the *Futuhat al-Makkiyya*, he writes:

> Through supererogatory works, God is the servant's hearing and seeing. Through obligatory works, the servant is the hearing and seeing of the Real, and by this is the cosmos established. . . . When the servant performs obligatory works, the fact that he is an attribute of the Real becomes manifest to him in them, but when he performs supererogatory works, the attribute of the Real belongs to him. Thereby the obligatory is differentiated from the supererogatory, and the higher degree belongs to the obligatory. [William Chittick, *The Sufi Path of Knowledge*, 1989, p330]

It's clear that Ibn al-'Arabi views the daily prayer and other obligatory works not so much as our action, but as God's action in us; consequently they have a reality beyond our subjective experience of them, a reality that is untouched by our personal understanding or the lack of it. Our potential understanding is an expression of possible being, whereas the rites themselves are an expression of Necessary Being. Nonetheless, a clear understanding of the symbolic meanings of the *namaz* may aid in the extension of the grace of Necessary Being—God—into the realm of possible being—which includes ourselves.

Viewed from this standpoint, *namaz* as a metaphysical meditation begins with an understanding of the symbols involved; unfolds to the point where the forms of the symbols disappear, leaving only their essential fragrance; and ends in a bare confrontation between humanity and God, between the symbolic manifestation of Reality and Reality Itself.

❖

When the time came for Junaid to die, he called for the water of ablution, and began the prostrations of *namaz*. 'O Chief of our Order,' cried his disciples, 'with all the works of obedience you have performed throughout your life and sent ahead of you, is this any time for prostration?' 'Never was Junaid in greater need than at this moment,' he answered.

# THE PRACTICE OF
# INVOCATION (*DHIKR*)

AUTHORITIES from many traditions have maintained that the Invocation of God's Name—the *dhikr* of the Sufis, the *mnimi Theou* of the Christian Hesychasts, the *japa-yoga* of the Hindus—is the appropriate spiritual practice for the latter days of this cycle of manifestation. Other practices can still be useful and effective; there will always be a place for personal prayer (whether of petition or of praise) and the canonical prayers of a given tradition (the Muslim *salat*; the Christian divine liturgy). Yet the cosmic environment of the planet and the energies of the psychic and the subtle-material planes have become so violent and chaotic in our times that intense psycho-physical practices such as *raja-yoga* or *kundalini-yoga* will undoubtedly find fewer and fewer practitioners able to withstand their rigors and bring them to a successful conclusion. The Invocation of the Name, on the other hand, possesses the virtues of simplicity, spiritual depth, and the ability to find a place in many different contexts, including solitary meditation, group practice, and the activities of daily life.

For the Invocation of the Name to become second nature, continuing even in sleep, is the proximate goal of the practice of it; nonetheless, the practice of Invocation must not become merely automatic or mechanical. According to Dr. Javad Nurbakhsh, the *dhikr* is not just some kind of internal tape recorder. One must both silently pronounce the Name, and also remember what it means. The word *Allah* must make present to us the *Reality* of Allah, otherwise we have turned the Name itself into an idol. And this encounter with the meaning of the Invocation cannot happen without a willing and conscious engagement of the Heart, which is both the spiritual center of the human psyche and the center-of-gravity of our conscious intent. The Heart, as a reality intrinsic to the human form, exists whether or not we are aware of it. And yet if we are not aware of it, it possesses only a virtual reality; in terms of our true spiritual condition, it is as if we had no Heart. If it did not pre-exist as a spiritual potential, we could never realize it: a Heart cannot be 'constructed' by the will and the conscious mind operating in a vacuum. And yet without a conscious and ongoing intent to focus upon it, this spiritual potential can never be actualized, and thus cannot properly be called a 'Heart'. The Heart is the unconscious root of our conscious attention; because God has first remembered us, He has made it possible for us to remember Him. When Meister Eckhart said, 'The eye through which God sees me, and the eye through which I see God, are the same eye', he was referring precisely to this mutual remembrance between man and God.

The Invocation of the Name of God is an ongoing act of willing and conscious attention, but it is also more than that. If it were not, if it depended upon nothing beyond raw self-will, it could never be constant, and would end by doing much more harm than good. According to authorities from many traditions, 'God and His Name are One'; in other words, it is possible for me to become conscious of God's Presence through the invocation of His Name only because God's Name *is* His Presence. If the Name were not the Presence, all our attempts to become aware of God's Presence by means of it would be futile; we would remain submerged in our own subjectivity. The Name is an objective factor, beyond our own habitual mental and emotional states; if it were not, it could in no way take our consciousness beyond these states, and place it in the objective Reality of God's Presence. (In Sufism, the sign of the Name's objectivity is the fact that it must be provided by a spiritual Master—just as, in Christianity, it has already been made available to all baptized Christians by their Master, Jesus Christ.) And yet, without the conscious and ongoing work of paying attention to both the Name and Its meaning, that objective Reality would remain veiled for us. This is another instance, or application, of the principle of the reciprocity between *Grace* and *works*. That God is objectively present, whether we attend to Him or not, is 'Grace'; that we can only receive this Grace by having faith in It, and then by attending to It, and finally by reaching certainty and stability with regard to It, is 'works'.

Invocation requires effort—and yet the whole of our effort is carried upon the great wave of ease and effortlessness and inevitability which is the sovereign Power of God. So *dhikr* is both laborious and effortless, both conscious and totally beyond our consciousness, both something we do and something that is done for us. As the Tibetan Buddhist teacher Chögyam Trungpa once put it, 'effort just comes to you.' Because of this dual quality of effort and effortlessness, the practice of Invocation is most naturally carried by the one human physical function which can be either voluntary or involuntary: the breath.

If God were not consciously attending to us and thus 'invoking our name' from all eternity, we would be completely unable to invoke His Name in the dimension of time (if for no other reason than that we would never have come into existence!). Thus the Invocation of the Name is both our willed and deliberate action, and also God's action within us. And while our action is forever incomplete and imperfect, God's action within us is complete and perfect, eternally and instantaneously. The central work of invoking the Name of God, therefore, must be for us to remember that He remembers us, to progressively leave behind our imperfect act of attention to Him, and place ourselves in the presence of His perfect attention to us. In the words of Muhammad, peace and blessings be upon him: 'Pray to God as if you saw Him, because even if you don't see Him, He sees you.'

The Name of God makes present to us the Reality of God, and one way it may do this is by gathering and synthesizing the knowledge of Himself that He has imprinted upon our Heart by means of the spiritual states He has sent us, each of which is paired with an 'intrinsic practice' proper to that state. For example, the recognition that God recreates the whole universe in every instant is naturally paired with the corresponding practice of letting oneself be completely transformed by Him, instant-by-instant, 'like a corpse in the hands of a washer of the dead'. The understanding that He is only imperfectly objective to me while I am perfectly objective to Him is paired with the practice of giving up trying to encompass God in knowledge while letting Him encompass me. And the feeling that God is absent (Absence being one of the modes of His Presence) is paired with a fierce longing to see His Face, ending in a resignation to His Will in either Presence or Absence, and a sacrifice of all willful attempts to command that Presence, in the recognition that they are only my human conceptions of Him, and thus nothing but idols. And these are only three examples of the innumerable modes in which He presents Himself to us in each spiritual moment, no two of which are alike. Some are capable of being partly expressed in words; others are far too subtle for any such expression. But unless the Invocation takes us beyond these 'contemplative unveilings' to the naked Presence of the Unveiled, it will degenerate into a rapid mental review of various bits of acquired philosophical knowledge, or an emotional melodrama of our love-affair with God, and the veil will fall again. What we already possess out of what God has given us is nothing; what He has yet in store for us is everything. And Who He Is in Himself is beyond even this everything. Love is beyond gratitude because gratitude veils Intimacy; Love is beyond hope because hope rejects Presence. 'When I came to Love,' said Rumi, 'I became ashamed of everything I ever said about Love.' Because God and His Name are One, only God has the power, and the right, to speak that Name. Spiritual states and their intrinsic practices comprise the shadow of lover cast upon the face of the Beloved—but when Love arrives, this shadow is nowhere to be seen.

# THE WAY OF PETITIONARY PRAYER (*MAS'ALAH*)

*Call upon Me in My Vision,*
*but do not petition Me;*
*petition Me in my absence,*
*but do not call upon me.*
Niffari

THOSE WEDDED to contemplative spirituality will sometimes look upon prayer of petition as beneath the station of gnosis, as something rendered unnecessary, if not rather *gauche*, by their (real or supposed) realization of the Pure Intellect. And it is certainly true that someone in whom the Absolute Witness is realized has already been given everything he or she could possibly want, and no longer conceives of God as a Divine Object to which petitions could be addressed. In the words of the famous woman Sufi Rabi'a al-Adawiyya, 'When the Heart is fully awake, it needs no Friend.'

It was the practice of certain great Sufis, like Rabi'a, never to ask for anything from anyone but God, and never ask God for anything except Himself. Here is a story about her that illustrates this point:

One day Rabi'a and her servant-girl were getting ready to break a fast of several days. The serving-girl needed an onion and was about to go next door and borrow one, but Rabi'a said: 'Forty years ago I vowed never to ask for anything from anyone but God—we can do without onions.'

Just then a bird flew over, and dropped an onion into Rabi'a's frying pan, peeled and ready to fry.

'Interesting but not convincing,' she said. 'Am I supposed to believe that God is an onion-vender? I mean, really.'

That day they fried their bread without onions.

Nonetheless, we do not all have the intimacy with God enjoyed by a great saint like Rabi'a. To emulate the saints, even if we know we have not attained to their station, can be a powerful spiritual practice; but for many of us, to reject God's onion may actually be to reject God Himself. To make light of His gifts because we want to pridefully pretend that we are without mundane needs (or perhaps because we secretly doubt that God can actually fulfill these needs) may in fact be the height of discourtesy.

Until God as *Al-Mujib*, the Answerer of Prayers, has fully dawned upon us, all of us harbor deep and unfulfilled desires. It is usual in the spiritual life to look upon such desires—to the degree that we are aware of them—as elements of selfishness and passion. But the truth is that our deepest desires are actually implanted in us by God, as ways through which we can come nearer to Him. We think we want a good meal, a good job, a fine house or an expensive car, a beautiful and generous lover—but God knows that what we really want, whether we know it or not, is Him. To ask for the satisfaction of a vice is to settle for much less than the fulfillment of a legitimate desire such as financial or emotional security; to ask for worldly security is to lack the imagination, if not the audacity, to ask for something much greater, such as spiritual illumination and wisdom; and to settle for spiritual states or even metaphysical wisdom when God is offering us His very Presence is truly to 'look a gift-horse in the mouth'.

In order to walk the path of petitionary prayer, we need to be honest about what we really want. If we can truly sacrifice a desire, then all the better. But if prayer and self-discipline have not been able to remove from us the desire for an object that is not overtly sinful, this may in fact mean that God is prompting us to ask for the fulfillment of that desire directly from Him. We must first admit the full depth of our desire for a particular object or outcome; then we must release that desire into God's hands, hoping that He will fulfill it according to our own conception, but at the same time saying, in all sincerity, 'not my will but Thine be done.' If we don't sacrifice our most cherished desire before the power of God's will, nothing of spiritual value will come of it—but if we don't admit the depth of that desire, then we will have nothing of value to sacrifice. Sacrifice is the harvest, but desire is the seed. Ibrahim ibn Adhem gave up the kingship of Balkh to pursue the Sufi path; because he was granted something great in worldly terms, he had the opportunity of making a sacrifice that was great in eternal terms, and thereby reaching an exalted spiritual station. If he had simply thought of his kingship as a burden, a worldly distraction that he was glad to get rid of, his sacrifice would have counted for little. He must have really wanted to be king of Balkh—but he wanted God more.

In answer to our prayer (and all true prayers are always answered) God may give us exactly what we've asked for, in the knowledge that we really need it—not for our physical or psychological security, necessarily, but for our spiritual receptivity and balance. He may withhold what we've asked for, in order to transmute, through purgatorial suffering, our desire for that object directly into a desire for Him. And He may also give us something unexpectedly different from and greater than the thing we asked for, something that is in fact much more appropriate and satisfying to our real needs than the thing we thought we wanted. (And if our prayer was not honest, He may send us circumstances that exactly mirror that dishonesty, so that, in undergoing them, we will be brought face to face with our own hypocrisy: *God is the best of plotters.*) But if we are serious about petitionary prayer as an element of the spiritual Path, we will need three things: the honesty to admit our deepest desires; the audacity to ask God to fulfill them; and the faith to believe that whatever is given by the All-Merciful and All-Compassionate, no matter how well it may match or how radically it may depart from our expectations, is best for us.

In relation to petitionary prayer, Jesus taught: 'Seek and you will find, ask and it will be given to you, knock and the door will be opened to you'; he recommended that we petition God like someone who pounds on a friend's door at midnight, asking to borrow bread to feed his guests (his spiritual states, his pure intentions). He taught us not only to ask God for things but to *importune* Him, to make a bloody nuisance of ourselves. But when he came to the eve of his crucifixion, his only prayer was: 'Father, if it is possible, let this cup pass from me; yet not my will, but Thine, be done.' The highest form of petitionary prayer is the one that is completely purified of any image of a desired or potential outcome. The gnostic does not ask God to change his eternal destiny, but to bring him more consciously and completely into the field of it. As the Prophet Muhammad prayed (peace and blessings be upon him), 'O God, show me things as they really are.'

# ON THE GREATER *JIHAD*

## (*Mostly From Correspondence*)

THE *nafs* (in the sense of 'soul') is composed of thought, will and feeling. Once we know what is true *intrinsically*, on the level of the Eye of the Heart, via Intellection or *ma'rifa*, or through Divine Revelation, it is comparatively easy to conform thought to Truth, to know what is true on a mental level. It is much more difficult to conform the will to Truth, to *follow* and *enact* what we know to be true in the abstract. And the hardest of all is to conform the feelings to the will, not only to know what is true, and to do what is true, but to love what is true. If the thought is conformed to *ma'rifa* or Revelation and the will conformed to thought, then the feelings eventually will follow—unless they are so strongly attached to dispersion that they begin to weaken and undermine the will. The feelings can be seen as the effective *fuel* of the will, which is why it is so difficult to will in opposition to our feelings. Still, only a will that can conform itself to Truth in opposition to the feelings can truly be called *will*. In the fallen soul, the will conforms itself to the feelings and the lower desires, and thought conforms itself to will, limiting itself to scheming how those desires can be fulfilled and how their fulfillment can be excused and rationalized. In the redeemed soul, the reverse is true: feelings follow will, will follows thought, and thought follows Truth. But the will can never reach its full effective power and unity unless the feelings follow. In response to this difficulty, one aspect of spiritual method is to appeal to the feelings directly, apart from the will, given the power of the feelings to mirror different realities. This is the use of sacred art, particularly (in a Sufi context) music and poetry. Of course the response of the feelings to the Beauty and Majesty of God, without the engagement of the will submitted to God's will, is unreliable; in love with God one day, they can be attracted to Marilyn Manson the next. But to 'educate' the feelings to respond to angelic and Divine influences *concurrently* with a training of the will to follow religious and spiritual practices has a much better chance of dislodging the feelings from inappropriate objects and making them submissive to the submitted will. When this process is complete, we can say that the *nafs*-at-peace has been realized. As a member of the Baby Boom generation, I certainly remember how it was to go to see some guru one day and sing heartfelt *kirtan* to Krishna, and the next day light up a joint and get off on listening to the Rolling Stones sing 'Midnight Rambler' or 'Sympathy for the Devil'. We are now living in the midst of the dire cultural effects of this sort of contradiction. As a poet, I adopted a kind of aesthetic morality which maintained (legitimately, on one level), that a poem was 'good' if it was aesthetically successful, and that it was illegitimate to condemn a 'good' poem because simply it was immoral. To be shocked at Baudelaire's *Flowers of Evil* would not have led to 'legitimate' literary criticism, besides being insufferably unhip! However, literary criticism has a very tenuous relationship to the spiritual life, apart from the fact that there is no longer time for it. In the midst of aesthetic or sexual glamour it is very hard to ask the question 'what is the ultimate end of all this fascination'? Yet we must ask it. If there is any use to aesthetic catholicity, which (in William Blake's words) talks with both angels and devils, it is to take us on a guided tour of our own soul; this is what seeking 'experience' of any kind is ultimately for. We need to know what our unredeemed, natural soul likes and dislikes, what it is capable of, and what it is entirely incapable of without God's help. Without this kind of direct self-knowledge, we are in danger of building our spiritual life on a shaky foundation of repressed, unconscious desires. But once this 'inventory' is complete, then we need to get to work strengthening virtue, transmuting the passions from unlawful expressions into lawful ones (from *subhuman* expressions to *human* ones), and eliminating those infernal elements which are pure negation, and as such have no right to exist. But how will we know when this inventory is complete? The possibilities of experience, the tendencies in our soul to identify with this and that, are effectively endless on their own level. Only the *baraka* of the spiritual path can present us with a real end to them. When the *tariqa* is entered, then the *nafs* constellates as something *apart from* and *opposed to* who we really are, as the *nafs al-ammara*. At this point, the Greater Jihad is begun, and we have no choice except—with God's help, and never without that help—to fight it through.

❖

After the Intellect has become veiled through *ghaflah*—heedlessness or ignorance—when a man who looks within his own soul he now sees the main thing, the highest thing, to be his individual will. Islam was sent to reverse the effects of the fall by teaching the submission of the individual will to God's Will—after which it becomes possible to see, in God, higher realities even than the Divine Will, exalted though that be. To submit to God is to begin to know Him; the pacification of the turbulent self-will unveils the Intellect and opens the Eye of the Heart.

❖

Asceticism is necessary but not sufficient for the spiritual Path. We need to go to war with the passions, with what the Sufis call the *nafs al-ammara;* but if we fight this battle with our own resources and in our own name, then we will lose. The ego with its self-will cannot overcome the passions, because self-will is a passion in itself, perhaps the greatest one. Only God can conquer the *nafs*—which is why, if we wait until we have subdued the lower soul before practicing the presence of God, we may well wait forever. We want to appear before God bathed and manicured, in our suit and tie; and this is a worthy desire in the face of God's majesty. But the other side of this desire is that we foolishly believe we can hide our impurities from Omniscience; we believe this because we want at all costs to avoid the *shame* of the encounter between our sinful souls and *Al-Quddus*, the Holy. Yet that shame is in itself a spiritual virtue. If the Physician is to heal us, we will have to 'come clean' with regard to our disease.

❖

Holy War is by God's command alone. Jihad is that moment when God commands us to draw the sword of purified anger against all that is not Himself; as Blake and the alchemists say, 'whatever *can* be destroyed *must* be destroyed!' Whoever arrogates to him- or herself, whether by claimed personal merit or by the sanction of collective sentiment, the right to proclaim Jihad is in the outer darkness *now*—but whoever, when God proclaims Jihad, refuses or hides from this call, will be pierced by God in battle. The war against all that is other than God is holy because it is initiated and carried to conclusion by the power of a Peace 'too great for the eye of man'. But when the sword is drawn, it encounters no alien flesh, it meets no enemy: because only God is.

❖

The King of the Jinn once told me:
'You don't draw your sword—
God draws *you*.'

# II

## RESPONSES

You insulted me, and I was happy;
Now that you've taken to flattering me,
May God Almighty forgive you.
Bitter words are more appropriate
Coming from that red, succulent,
sugar-greedy lip.

[*after Hafiz*]

# SEPARATION

He is there
and I am here.
There is neither a path nor
a wall between us,
and I am paralyzed
by my own uselessness.
If you go to war against me,
my Friend,
with your great strength
I may somehow find the
strength to follow…
—that's why I
taunt You.

# EMBRACING THE FIRE

The Fire is kindled;
Hear it seethe and crackle.
Suffering is the Fire:
Remembrance fans the flames.
Remembrance is the Fire,
Suffering the fuel that feeds it.
My wandering attention
Lights like a fool on
This or that perishing thing—
Remembrance calls it home:
Home to the Fire.
My heart is the altar,
Remembrance the Fire,
My living flesh the sacrifice.
Every nest on this world's tree:
Thrown into the Fire.
No perch. No resting-place.
No home.
Don't let the Fire starve.
Never let it die.
Bring more suffering.
Bring more fuel.
What would not wish
To pass through that Fire
And become immortal?
Come, fear of death.
Come, terror of failure.
Come, grim loneliness.
Come, weight of the world.
To feel pain is to suffer;
To suffer is to bear;

To bear is to allow;
To allow is to prevail.
The Fire speaks the Name.
The Fire is the burning Name
Of Him Who speaks it.
Beaten on the anvil of it
I take the single shape
That is His will.
Sweet Fire. Pungent knowledge.
Fragrant wood-smoke
Leads the vigilant, listening world
Back to the Heart of the Fire.

# GRATITUDE

Thank you, God, for being God.
Thank you for not leaving that job to me
To be the puppet of my own faithlessness,
An incompetent, fumbling creator
Who somehow knew how to make a world
But never learned how to govern it.
What I will do, You have already done;
Where I must fail, You can never fail.
That we don't all die the first time we
      fall asleep
But wake together in the common morning
As if we had never been obliterated
Is conclusive proof of both Your existence,
      and our need.
O God, thank you for the gift of my need.

# INSIDE GOD

Inside God
There is the sound of distant traffic,
The smell of rose incense,
And one cricket.
Inside God
Somebody keeps leaving and returning
With the rhythm of the breath.
He was never really here,
And so he never really left.
Inside God
Someone is listening through the ear
And things are listening to themselves.
Across the marsh
A young dog is barking.
The cricket starts, then stops.
Inside God
Everything becomes part of the world.
No one is looking at this world,
And yet the world is clearly seen.
Inside God
The mystery that Someone could be
Without starting waves
Without making declarations
Is the quality of the autumn wind,
Of a truck changing gears,
Of children playing.
A gap in the flow
Of things naming themselves,
The dog barking '*dog*',
The child screaming '*child*',
Is the place of the Name.

Here, He says, is the Friend you were searching for
Looking out through your eyes
Upon currents of laughter
And motionless objects, somberly involved
In the act of being.
He Who is no-one
Is the very One
Who lets all these things be.
The cricket chirps '*God*'.
Inside God
I was a small object seen on the horizon.

# III

## COSMIC REFLECTIONS OF
## THE METAPHYSICAL ORDER

What plot do you keep in the tip of your curl
That makes you let down, once more, the flood
Of that perfumed hair?
If you keep my head spinning in the circle of
what might be,
I will never begin to know the mysteries
Of what must be.

                    [*after Hafiz*]

# NATURE, ART, AND ALCHEMY

THE IMAGE OF HUMANITY as the destroyer of nature is so over-whelming in our time that we have forgotten the traditional doctrine that man is the perfecter, and also the perfection, of the natural order. A western Muslim equestrienne and scholar of horse-manship, particularly of the Arabian contribution to European horse-training, was once heard to say: 'Whoever sees a finely-bred and well-trained Spanish horse next to a wild mustang, no matter how ignorant of horse breeding he or she is, will recognize at a glance that the blood horse is the more beautiful of the two. Horsemanship is a spiritual art, because to train a horse correctly, so that animal and rider respond as one, is also to train one's *nafs*—not by grossly dominating it, but by teaching it to follow, willingly, the human spirit that rules it.' *And [it is He who creates] horses and mules and asses for you to ride, as well as for beauty; and He will yet create things of which you have no knowledge.* (Q. 16:8) This passage may indicate, among other things, the transformation, through perfect submission to God, of the commanding self or headstrong ego into the self-at-peace. It may also refer to the body which will be ours after the Resurrection. The human-headed horse named *Buraq* which, according to legend, the Prophet rode on his *miraj*, is an symbol of the self-at-peace.

This is alchemy: man is both the substance to be refined, and the crucible; God is both the Refiner, and the Fire.

Al-Ghazali classified alchemy as among the 'intellectual sciences'; unlike such things as magic and sorcery, it is permissible to Muslims. We usually think of alchemy as an early precursor to chemistry, and that's certainly true as far as it goes. But there is more to this craft than simple chemistry. According to Seyyed Hossein Nasr (who, besides being a master of Islamic history and doctrine, earned a degree from the Massachusetts Institute of Technology), in his *Islamic Science: An Illustrated Study*,

...a few practicing alchemists were reported early in [the 20<sup>th</sup>] century in such areas as the Maghrib. But few realize that in those centers of the Islamic world where the traditional arts are still alive—in such cities as Yazd and Isfahan in Persia—alchemy still survives on a much larger scale than is outwardly suspected. Its dispensations...make the continuity of such arts as the weaving of traditional cloth possible.

A few real masters of the art survive along with many amateurish aspirants. The masters are well-hidden and usually veil their activity by some kind of outward occupation such as shopkeeping or the practice of medicine. Yet they are not wholly inaccessible to those who really seek them. To meet with one of these masters is to be faced with the blinding evidence that alchemy is not simply a proto-chemistry, for in their presence one feels not as if one were in the presence of an ordinary chemistry teacher but as if one were bathing in the sun on a cool autumn day. They exhibit a spiritual presence, intelligence and inner discipline which proves that they are concerned above and beyond all charcoal-burning with the transformation of the base metal of the soul and the unveiling of the gold or the sun which shines at the center of man's being, were he only to lift the veil which eclipses it before the outer eye. (pp 204–205)

In the history of Islam, alchemy has always been related to the traditional crafts, to medicine, and to art. As to the question of whether base metal can really be transmuted into gold, on rare occasions, by alchemists in their workshops, it was always debated and has not yet been settled. What we can be sure of is that the symbols and metaphors of alchemy relate directly to the purification and integration of the human soul—which means that in one of its aspects, alchemy is a form of traditional psychotherapy. In this special psychotherapy, however, unlike the modern brand, we do not 'adjust' to society or our natural passions, but to our *fitrah*, the eternal form of Humanity in the mind of God.

The spiritual secret of any traditional craft is: as nature is shaped and refined, so is human nature. As every traditional craft is also an art, so every art is also a craft; it is an alchemy which works to synthesize beauty and use, just as they are synthesized in virgin nature, or in the normal human body, and thereby purge the soul of the grossness or capriciousness that could conceive of an ugly usefulness, or a useless beauty. That so much of what modern society produces in the name of usefulness is so ugly, and that so much it produces in the name of beauty is actually useless—as well as being, in many cases, far from beautiful—shows how far society has departed from the sound spiritual principles upon which Islam is based.

A key concept in alchemy, which is derived from (or through) Aristotle, is the polarity between *matter* and *form*. Form is the true essence or spirit of something; matter (in the traditional, not the modern sense), is the formless, receptive field where that form manifests. Like a mirror, it has no form of its own, but impartially reflects any form that comes near it. In the case of a lion made of gold, the *lion* is the form and the *gold* is the matter.

The idea, in alchemy, is to bring the two together, so that form is actualized and matter spiritualized. An automobile is more organized and useful than a collection of automobile parts; a house is more complete, more fully realized, than a pile of bricks. When a field is ploughed and sown and fertilized, when iron is extracted from ore and transformed into steel by the addition of carbon, a kind of alchemy is being done. Alchemy works with nature to transform nature, to bring it to a higher level of organization, closer to form, closer to spirit.

All of us have ideas or plans or aspirations which are not yet realized. We also have capacities and resources which have not yet been put to use. To realize an idea is to embody a *form*; to put one's resources (which are related to *matter*) into the service of a form or an idea is to wake them up, to bring them out of chaos, to raise them to a higher level. Whether you are making a copper pot or writing a computer program or starting a business or developing your character, you will always need both a *plan* to follow and the *resources* to finish the work. The more completely you can bring these two together, in both the spiritual and practical parts of your life, the closer you will come to deserving the name of 'human being'. And besides the plan and the resources, one more thing is needed: the wisdom, the skill and the character-strength to unite them. In alchemical terminology, which uses the properties of certain metals and chemicals to symbolize the basic elements needed to complete any kind of work, the *plan* might correspond to Sulfur, the *resources* to Mercury, and *wisdom and character-strength* to Salt.

Perhaps the central concept in Islamic philosophy is the polarity between essence (*mahiyya*) and being (*wujud*), which is something like the polarity between form and matter, but on a higher level. Almost every major Muslim philosopher—al-Farabi, Ibn Sina, Mulla Sadra—has dealt in one way or another with the question of essence and being. Now as many have pointed out, the danger in philosophy is that it can go off on its own and depart from the truths of revealed religion, as it did in the Christian West with disastrous consequences. Al-Ghazali, in his *The Incoherence of the Philosophers*, prevented Islamic philosophy from doing this. Some say he destroyed Islamic philosophy; the truth is, he placed it firmly under the rule of religion. His own writings are filled with elements derived from the Greek philosophers, but he always put religion first. He did not destroy philosophy; he conquered it, and incorporated it into Dar al-Islam. And as long as philosophy serves religion, and doesn't pretend to be able to discover the truths of God by reason alone outside of what is revealed to us in the Qur'an, it can sometimes help us get an inkling of the nature and reality of God—for those who have philosophical minds, that is, which not everyone does, or needs to; the self-sacrifice of the martyr, the faith of the *mumin* is a much greater virtue than the subtle philosophical understanding of a coward or an unbeliever. According to traditional Islamic philosophy, for example, being and essence are only partially united in the forms of the world; in God are they perfectly united. In the single case of God, Who is the Unique (*al-Wahid*), *what* He is (His essence) is identical with *the fact that* He is (His being).

Being is the 'isness' of things; essence is the 'whatness' of things. That a rock *is* is its being; that a rock is a rock, and nothing else, is its essence. Now this way of thinking will sound to many people like a meaningless mental exercise. After all, since no thing exists that has being without essence (since it wouldn't be anything) or essence without being (since it wouldn't be), and given that being and essence can only be separated within the mind, then why separate them? Why, except to create an empty illusion?

The answer to this question, or one answer, is—in the words of William Blake—'to cleanse the doors of perception'. If you drive by an oak tree that you've whizzed past a thousand times before, you will tend not to really see it; you will take it for granted. But if one day you were to see an oak tree, normal in every way except that it was hanging in mid-air, it would rivet your attention. You would see it in dazzling clarity and incandescent detail. The 'real' tree was of no particular interest to you, but this 'unreal' tree, this *apparitional* one—how vivid it is; how *real*.

The alchemy of being and essence is to separate them within the mind, and then reunite them on a higher level. This separation and reunion is what all true art does, to break us free from our stale habits of perception. In a classical Persian miniature, the images of the rocks, the trees, the birds, the human figures take place in a magical world of their own, in what is called the Imaginal Plane, the *alam al-mithal*, the world where eternal truths appear as living beings, as they often do in dreams. The great Persian painter creates this impression simply by removing the literal *being* of his subject, and leaving only the *essence*. What was once given existence by air and water and wood and stone is now embodied in the existence of paint and panel. His painting is obviously not a reproduction of nature, like a painting by a 'realistic' or 'naturalistic' artist; the perspective is collapsed, for one thing, so that everything appears as if woven into a carpet or painted on a screen. It is made like this so that it will appear *as* an apparition, an image, not an imitation or counterfeit of the 'real thing', which Islam forbids as a form of idolatry. This is how it reveals the *essence* of its subject, so that, when we find ourselves walking through a land of rocks and trees, the trees filled with singing birds, and happen to recall the image of a Persian miniature, the imaginary landscape and the 'real' one may unexpectedly merge in our consciousness. When this happens, the landscape suddenly becomes transparent—not to sunlight or human vision, but to *meaning*. The world appears not as a set of material objects and forces, but as a pattern composed of the living signs of God's presence. *Wherever you turn, there is the face of God.*

If we always think we know *what* things are, we may forget to realize *that* they are. Our world will become matter-of-fact, boring, literal—opaque to the Light of God. This is a state of mind the alchemists symbolized by *lead,* where being and essence, or Source (God) and His manifestation (nature) are chaotically mixed or crushed together. In the art of alchemy, these two must first be separated, and then reunited in a higher level, so that essence *reveals* being instead of hiding it; this is what is meant by the alchemical recipe *solve et coagula,* 'dissolve, then coagulate'. This higher union of being and essence produces the condition that the alchemists call *gold*; when we see nature as composed of nothing but the signs of God, then we live in a *golden world.* To stop viewing the world as a materialistic machine and start seeing it as a carpet woven with the mysterious signs of God is to transmute lead into gold.

This is the alchemy which all true art serves. As the human substance is purified through the remembrance of God, nature becomes a vision of the signs of God. And as our vision of nature is refined through art, the human substance is refined as well, so that it can more perfectly reflect its Divine Source. The world around us is transformed into the Walled Garden, the image of Paradise.

# THE SIGNS OF GOD IN
# MATHEMATICS & GEOMETRY

## *An Islamic Perspective*

### I

IN ISLAMIC DOCTRINE, God is said to be both incomparable (*tanzih*), and also capable of being compared (*tashbih*) with various aspects of the created world—at least up to a point. In English terminology, *tanzih* is God's *transcendence*, while *tashbih* is His *immanence*. Without *tashbih*, the signs of God could not appear in nature; without *tanzih*, nature would literally be God. In the *surah al-Fatihah* God is called Lord of the Worlds, Owner of the Day of Judgment. He is compared to a great and powerful man. This is *tashbih*. In the *surah al-Ikhlas*, it is said that He neither begets nor is begotten, and there is nothing to which He can be compared. This is *tanzih*.

Both *tanzih* and *tashbih* are reflected in the world of mathematics. Pythagoras, Plato and their followers believed that mathematics and the various sciences based on it—music, geometry, etc.—were the best possible preliminary training for the understanding of eternal truths. This view of mathematics was inherited, and even further developed, by the philosophers and scientists of Islam. According to Seyyed Hossein Nasr,

Any first-hand knowledge of Islamic civilization and particularly the Islamic sciences reveals the 'privileged position' of mathematics in the Islamic tradition. There are crystalline and geometric aspects to Islamic art and architecture, a love of arithmetic and numerical symbolism in both the plastic and auditory arts—especially poetry and music—an 'algebra' of language and of thought so clearly reflected in Arabic and also in many other Islamic languages, and numerous other tangible manifestations which make plain the central role of traditional mathematics in Islamic art and civilization and on the highest level in the spiritual 'style' of Islam so directly reflected in its sacred art.

This love for mathematics, especially geometry and number, is directly connected to the essence of the Islamic message, which is the doctrine of Unity (*al-tawhid*). God is One; hence the number one in the series of numbers is the most direct and intelligible symbol of the Source. And the series of numbers themselves is a ladder by which man ascends from the world of multiplicity to the One. (*Islamic Science: An Illustrated Study*, p75)

Just as the eternal principles or Names of God are reflected in mathematics, so mathematical principles and relationships are reflected directly in nature: in the structure of atoms and crystals, in the design of cells, flowers and other living things, in the orbits of the planets and the revolutions of the galaxies—in fact, in virtually anything we can investigate.

Michael Denton, author of *Nature's Destiny*, has remarked on the seemingly miraculous fitness of mathematics, an entirely abstract science, for understanding the concrete realities of nature, and on the equally miraculous fitness of the human mind and brain to invent mathematics, and apply it to that kind of understanding.

One of the things that William A. Dembski deals with in his book *Intelligent Design*, which is written to demonstrate that the universe is designed by an intelligent Agent, is the relationship between theology and science. He wants to reassure scientists that the role of theology is not to *stop* scientific inquiry by simply saying 'God made the universe and that's that,' but actually *to stimulate deeper and wider inquiry*—through purely scientific methods—by proving that the universe is in fact designed, and setting up exact mathematical criteria by which such design can be detected. In the following passage, Dembski uses mathematics as a metaphor for the precise way science and theology relate to each other, comparing the way of knowing things of naturalistic science to *rational numbers,* and the way of theology to *real numbers.*

In principle the applied mathematician can do everything he or she needs by working with rational numbers. Nevertheless it turns out that the mathematician's task becomes a lot easier when he or she embeds rational numbers into the real numbers and uses the real numbers to derive formulas and equations. The real numbers are known as the completion of the rational numbers.

The real numbers include both the rational numbers and the irrational numbers (these are numbers like $\pi$ and the square root of 2, written $\sqrt{2}$, which require for their representation infinite and nonrepeating decimal expansions). Thus in going to the real numbers, the applied mathematician loses nothing that he or she had before in the rational numbers. Nevertheless the real numbers are not an artificial addendum to the rational numbers. The rational numbers, even though adequate for all the actual calculations that the applied mathematician makes, are *conceptually inadequate.*

A circle whose radius is given by a rational number $q$ has a circumference given by the irrational number $2\pi q$. A square whose side has a length given by a rational number has a diagonal length given by the irrational number $\sqrt{2}\,s$. The applied mathematician will always end up in practice approximating $2\pi q$ and $\sqrt{2}\,s$ with rational numbers. But the fact remains that in assigning rational approximations to the circumference of a circle and the diagonal of a square, the applied mathematician cannot escape that these inevitably are approximation whose validity as approximations depends on the real numbers that complete the rational numbers. In calculating the circumference of a circle and the diagonal of a square, the applied mathematician is in the first place concerned with the actual circumference of that circle and the actual diagonal of that square, and not with their rational approximation. Rational approximations come afterward, being the best that applied mathematicians can do given their limitations as finite rational agents in a physical world. (pp 208–209)

In this passage we meet three different kinds of numbers: *Rational numbers* include both integers (the familiar whole numbers), and finite or repeating decimal expansions. 3 is an integer; 1/2 is a finite decimal (0.5); 1/3 is a repeating decimal (.3333333... etc.). Other numbers such as the decimal for 1/7 (.142857142857142857... etc.) are also repeating decimals. *Irrational numbers* are those which represent definite quantities or relationships, but which cannot be perfectly expressed in terms other than themselves. *Pi* ($\pi$) is the relationship of the radius of a circle to its circumference. It is obviously a definite relationship, as every specific instance of it is a definite quantity, yet there is no way it can be perfectly expressed as a number. The attempt to express it as a number results in the non-repeating decimal 3.14159265... etc. And then there are *real numbers*, which include both rational and irrational numbers.

Dembski compares rational numbers to the kind of knowledge science can discover, and real numbers to the kind of knowledge theology deals with. It's easy to see from his metaphor that the perspective of theology *must* include that of naturalistic science, but the perspective of naturalistic science *can never* include that of theology, though it can certainly provide theology with useful metaphors. (It is important to remember here that not all science is naturalistic; as Seyyed Hossein Nasr points out, there is such a thing as traditional or sacred science.) The relationship between the two can be compared to a two-storey house where the partition separating the first and second storeys is a one-way mirror. Looking upward from the bottom storey, it is a mirror; looking down from the upper storey, it is a transparent floor. Standing in the upper storey (theology) you can see into the lower one (science), but standing in the lower one you can never see into the upper one; all you can see is your own reflection.

The same three types of numbers can also be understood as signs of three different aspects of God, or of the relationship between God and His creation. Rational numbers are like *tashbih;* the aspect of quantity which can be expressed in rational numbers is like the quality of God by which He is comparable to various aspects of His creation. Quantities such as seven objects, or one-third of an object, have a direct, straightforward relationship to the object or objects we are counting or dividing. Irrational numbers, on the other hand, are like *tanzih.* God's absolute transcendence of the world is undoubtedly real; if He were limited to this or that aspect of the universe, or if He were simply identified with the universe as a whole, He would not be God. But this truth cannot be expressed in terms other than itself. In rational terms, it is not this, not that, not anything you can point to or name. In a non-repeating decimal, each number we add to the series as we try and come up with a numerical expression for the quantity in question is not only insufficient, it is also of no value in predicting what the next number will be. Only by continuing to work out the decimal can we know what the next number in the series will be—a number which will also be insufficient, and of no help in predicting the next number after that. Like God's action in the world and the human heart, each number appears, as it were, directly from the Unseen.

But *rational and irrational numbers together* make up the set of real numbers. If this were not the case, then rational numbers could be taken as symbols of the universe and irrational numbers as symbols of God, with no common ground between them—and so we would be in a condition of *shirk;* we would be treating the universe as if it were a second Reality, a partner to God. But since both rational and irrational numbers are real, real numbers can be taken as a symbol of God's Reality, which includes both His comparability (*tashbih*) and His incomparability (*tanzih*). If God were not real, and if He were not both comparable and incomparable, there would be no such things as real, rational and irrational numbers. Only theology or metaphysics, however, can see things from this perspective; naturalistic science cannot.

## II

The central doctrine of Islam is *al-tawhid*, Unity. God is One, there is no god but God. And the Unity of God is reflected in the universe as well, in the unity of nature's laws, as well as in the uniqueness of each object in nature.

To construct a circle is to make a geometrical diagram of *al-tawhid*. The *fatihat*, the opening *surah* of the Qur'an, is like an analysis of the doctrine of *al-tawhid*; the specific properties of the circle appear in the verses of the *fatihat*.

The point at the center of the circle is the point of Transcendent Unity—transcendent because a geometrical point is dimensionless. The center of a circle or the intersection of two lines define a given point—but without the circle, without the lines, the point is without location, invisible, unknowable. The *surah al-Ikhlas* describes God as incapable of being compared to anything at all. The same is true, in a way, of the geometrical point. Two points define a line, three points a flat surface, and four points a three-dimensional volume. But a single point, though it is the starting-point for any line, or plane, or volume, is not one among the objects of this world. This makes it an apt symbol for *tanzih*, the Transcendence of God.

As Michael S. Schneider points out in *A Beginner's Guide to Constructing the Universe*, when we use a compass and a piece of paper to expand the geometrical point into a circle by making 'one turn'— the literal meaning of the English word 'universe'—we are using geometry to illustrate God's act of creating the cosmos. But we are also, in a way, translating the *fatihat* into geometrical terms:

*Bismillah* ('in the Name of God') is the central point, the transcendent God.

*Ar-Rahman ar-Rahim* ('the Merciful, the Compassionate') is the circumference of the circle. *Ar-Rahman* is the Mercy by which God creates the universe; *ar-Rahim* is the Mercy by which He gathers it back to Himself. Together they make a complete cycle, or circle, of creation and return—the second of the three properties of the circle according to Michael Schneider. But here one might ask: Wouldn't the creation of the universe from God and its return to God be better represented as a kind of loop which starts at the original point and then returns to it? Yes, that might also be a useful and evocative symbol; it is one of the properties of symbolism that many different symbols can point to one and the same reality, from many different points of departure. An even better symbol would be the shape of an upside-down heart, where the point of beginning is the lower (now upper) point, from which existence expands and descends, until it reaches the invisible horizontal line where the two lobes of the heart begin to curve together, till they meet and form a single vertical line, which travels up through the inverted heart, back to the point of beginning. (*Qalb*, the Arabic word for 'heart', comes from the root QLB, whose meanings include both 'something *turned* upside-down' and 're*turn*'.)

But there are a number of reasons why the circumference of a circle also symbolizes the cycle of creation and return. One reason is that God is 'equidistant' (so to speak) from every point on the cycle; He is both *al-Zahir*, the Outward, and *al-Batin*, the Inward. In the words of the Qur'an, *Wherever you* turn, *there is the face of God.* Another is that the created world, *while it remains itself*, can never really return to God. God is the only Reality; whatever appears to exist in its own right, apart from God, can only 'orbit' Him; it can never become One with Him. Creation returns to God not by *blending* with Him, as if two real things had now become One thing (to believe this would be to ascribe a partner to God, the sin of *shirk*), but by being annihilated, until nothing remains *but* Him. A third is that, from God's point of view, the universe does not need to return to Him because it never really departed from Him. (In the words of the *hadith*, 'Before the creation, God was alone, without a second; and He is even now as He was.')

*Alhamdulillahi Rab el-alimin, ar-Rahman ar-Rahim* ('all praise be to God, Lord of the worlds'): Within the circumference (*ar-Rahman ar-Rahim*), connecting it with the central point, are an infinite number of radii. The radii symbolize the 'worlds' of which God (as the central point) is 'Lord'. This is the first property of the circle, according to Michael Schneider: equal expansion in all directions.

*Maliki yawmiddin* ('Owner of the Day of Judgment'): This phrase could be symbolized as a circle containing a spiral leading back to the central point, representing the collapse of the circumference into the center. Any single form—for example, a living human soul—moves in the cycle *ar-Rahman ar-Rahim*, from creation to return. But when the cycle itself collapses into the center, that is the Day of Judgment, the point where Transcendence has the final say. The King *(Rab)* rules, but the Owner *(Malik)* can liquidate. The Day of Judgment is the end of time, certainly, but it is more than that. It is also the realization that creation, in relation to God, in the face of the Absolute Reality, is as if it were nothing, even now. *All is perishing except His Face.* This is the corollary of the second property of the circle: whatever can expand in all directions can also contract in the same way.

*Iyyaka na budu wa iyyaka nastain* ('Thee alone do we worship, to Thee alone do we *turn* for help'): This is the third property of the circle, according to Schneider: that of enclosing the greatest space within the shortest perimeter. It is as if the widest possible expansion were enclosed within the greatest possible contraction, as in the case of the child within the mother's womb, or within the circle of the mother's love. The words *Rahman* and *Rahim*, usually translated as 'mercy' and 'compassion', both come from an Arabic root which means 'womb'. This is God's intrinsic protection of all beings in the embrace of His own nature. We worship That outside of which there is nothing; we turn for help to That which surrounds us, whichever way we turn. In the words of the Qur'an, *Wherever you turn, there is the Face of God.*

*Ihdinas sirat al-mustaqim, sirat al-lazina anamta alayhim; ghayril maghzubi alayhem wa laz zaallin* ('guide us on the straight path, the path of those you have blessed, not those who have earned your anger, or those who have gone astray'): The straight path is the radius—not just any radius, but the line which travels from where I really am, from my unique point on the circumference of God's creation, from my life not as I fear it is, or hope it is, but as it genuinely is, straight to the center, the One. At the end of time, on the Day of Judgment, the circle will collapse. My duty is to travel the straight path to the Center *before* the Day of Judgment overtakes me. In the words of the Prophet (peace and blessings upon him), 'die before you are made to die.' In geometrical terms, the rightly-guided are traveling toward the Center on a *radius*. But those who have earned God's anger or who have gone astray are traveling on a *chord* instead—a line which leads from one point on the circumference to another without passing through the center, which ends at a point that is neither one's genuine starting-place nor one's true destination. This is how one becomes a 'trespasser'.

The Arabic word for 'heart', *qalb*, is derived from the root QLB or QBL, which embraces a number of concepts having to do with 'turning'. In Islamic metaphysics the Heart is the center of the psyche, the point at which it is intersected by the vertical ray of the

Spirit (*ruh*). This symbolic image has obvious affinities with the act of constructing a circle using compass and a sheet of paper. The Heart is who we really are in the sight of God; it is the central point of our full and authentic humanity. Whoever wants to rise along the vertical path of the Spirit, the *axis mundi*, first has to have reached the Center, the Heart, which is another way of saying that we can't relate to God with only a part of ourselves. A line drawn from any point on the circumference of a circle so as to intersect a line passing vertically through the circle's center can never be one with the infinite elevation which the vertical line defines. It must intersect the vertical line at some point short of infinity. Furthermore, it only 'represents' its own point-of-origin on the circumference; it can in no way stand for the circle as a whole. But the center of the circle does stand for whole circle, since it is the point from which the circle expands, and to which it returns. And only the central point of the circle is available to the ray of infinite elevation which symbolizes the relationship between the human being and God. It is said that God holds the Heart between His fingers, and turns it however He will. This is a way of saying that the Heart is the reality through which we can see how all the changes-of-state we experience in passing time have the same Point-of-Origin; that change on the horizontal plane is an expression of permanence on the vertical one; that the *waqt*, the present moment of spiritual time, is the manifestation of God's eternity in the created world. And just as God *turns* the Heart however He will, so the Heart is the point through which and by which the human soul *returns* to God on the spiritual Path; it is the spiritual Kaaba, the *qiblah* toward which we turn.

# ALCHEMY AS
# SPIRITUAL PSYCHOTHERAPY

## With an Exegesis of the
## Eastern Orthodox Icon of St. George

IN THE HEALTHY SOUL, the affections are in harmony with the will, the will with the rational mind, and all three with the transcendent Intellect. It is also necessary for us, however, to have a clear image of the condition of the sick or fallen soul, as well as the method by which this soul can be healed. This image and method can be found in the science of alchemy—which, among traditional sciences, most directly corresponds to 'psychotherapy' in the strict sense of the word (though certainly not to many modern practices which go by that name).

In the alchemical art, the goal is to forge 'the Philosopher's Stone' or 'the alchemical gold', through a marriage of Sulfur and Mercury in the context of Salt, which acts as a catalyst. The main stages of the Work are *melanosis*, 'blackening'; *leucosis*, 'whitening'; and *iosis*, 'reddening'. Blackening is radical humility and self-mortification, symbolized by the metal lead. Whitening is virginal receptivity to the light of the Spirit, symbolized by silver. Reddening signalizes the completion of the Work, the attainment of the Philosopher's Stone whereby the body is spiritualized and the Spirit embodied. It represents the establishment of permanent psychic stability under the rule of the Spirit; it is symbolized by gold.

According to Titus Burckhardt, in his *Alchemy: Science of the Cosmos, Science of the Soul* and the chapter 'Insight into Alchemy' in his *Mirror of the Intellect: Essays on Traditional Science & Sacred Art*, Sulfur is the Spirit, Mercury the soul, and Salt the body. However, it is more strictly accurate to call Sulfur 'Spirit as reflected in the soul,' since alchemy, as one of the lesser mysteries, is properly a psychic art. And the elusive quality of Mercury, as well as the acrid, volatile and inflammatory quality of Sulfur, also make them apt symbols of the various powers of the soul *in their fallen condition*. If Sulfur and Mercury were not fallen in some sense, and therefore estranged, their union would not represent the purification and re-ordering of the soul.

Specifically, unredeemed Sulfur symbolizes *rationality in bondage to the will*, and unredeemed Mercury *will in bondage to the affections*. When the rational mind is bound to the will, it becomes 'sulphurous': dry, explosive, volatile, self-willed, and filled with fixed ideas. It believes not what the transcendent Intellect reveals as true, but what it arbitrarily decides to believe. Likewise when will is bound to the affections, it becomes 'mercurial': manipulative and capricious, seductive and yet 'playing hard to get'. It does not do what the rational mind demonstrates it ought to do, but only what it wants to do at the moment. Thus fallen Sulfur is in some ways like the character of an immature man, fallen Mercury like that of a childish woman. If the healthy or 'edified' soul (edified in the sense of 'built up', as in our word 'edifice') is hierarchicalized with the rational mind at the highest level, as interpreter of the Intellect, the will at the mid-level, as servant of the Intellect, and the affections at the lowest level, as receptive mirror of the Intellect, in the fallen soul this hierarchy is inverted: the affections rule the will; the will rules the rational mind; the Intellect is veiled.

The alchemical cure for the 'sickness' of Sulfur and Mercury, the power which brings them together, is, in the terminology of Sufism, *taslim*: submission to God. *taslim* is Salt, the simplest and most basic truth of things, as when we call someone 'the salt of the earth'. Salt is the matrix, the alchemical vessel, the *context* which allows Sulfur and Mercury to marry. And although Salt is usually identified as the principle of the body, it is, mysteriously, also a symbol of the Divine Essence, since submission to God puts us in direct touch with the Absolute Itself. As the marriage of Spirit and soul takes place within the context of the body, so the union of Truth and Love subsists within the context of the Essence. What is highest is best symbolized by what is lowest; the relative stability of the material world more perfectly reflects the Absolute than do the shifting images of the psyche—even though, ontologically speaking, they are closer to it. This is why the alchemists teach that the first prerequisite for the alchemical *magnum opus* is the heaviest and most material of the metals known to classical antiquity—lead. In Islamic terms, the union of Spirit and soul in humanity, reflecting the unity of Truth and Love in the Divine Essence, is related to the doctrine of the *insan al-kamil*; the Perfect or Universal Man. In Christian terms, it has to do with the mystery of the Incarnation. (NOTE: The identification of Salt as submission-to-God with the Divine Essence is my own. The only traditional source I can cite to support it is *The Psychology of Sufism* by Dr. Javad Nurbakhsh, page 66, where salt is listed among the symbols of the '*nafs*-at-peace', the human soul submitted to God, and where one of the symbolic meanings of salt in dreams and visions is given as 'submissiveness'.)

On the psychic level, where the metaphors of alchemy apply, knowledge of God, love of God, and the will to follow God's Will as we understand it are all necessarily imperfect, since they are mediated by the limited human subject. Submission alone is virtually perfect, since in reality nothing happens outside God's Will; consequently all things, whether or not they *have* submitted, in essence *are* submitted. When the will submits to God, the rational mind, freed from the will's domination, becomes objective and impartial—obedient to the Intellect—while the will itself, since it is now submissive to a higher Principle, is freed from the domination of the affections, which in turn submit to it. So the true hierarchy is re-established in the soul. Here the initial need of the will, in obedience to the rational mind, to battle against the unruly emotions of the passional soul, which Sufis call the *nafs al-ammara*, 'the commanding self', is replaced by a state in which emotions gladly submit to the will, and lend to it the fullness of their power. (NOTE: In Sufism, the human soul goes through several stages of alchemical transformation in the course of the spiritual Path. It begins as 'the commanding *nafs*' or passional soul, is transformed through spiritual struggle into 'the accusing *nafs*'—the remorseful conscience—and ends by becoming 'the *nafs*-at-peace', the purified soul obedient to God's will.)

❖

The story of this 'war against the soul' and the alchemical trans-mutation it produces, is told—in the language of images—in one version of the Orthodox Christian icon of St. George (who, interest-ingly, is identified by Sufis with the 'immortal prophet' Khidr or Khezr, the Green One, their hidden patron). St. George, mounted on a horse, with an angel above him holding a crown over the saint's head, impales a dragon with his lance, the opposite end of which points upward toward the angel, whose face is like a minia-ture prototype of the saint's. The dragon seems to be lying on a body, not of ice, but of solid glassy-green water. In the background is a tower where, from the battlements, a king, a queen and a prince are watching the contest. In front of the tower stands a princess—who, like Andromeda or Psyche, has presumably been given to the dragon to devour. She holds in her hand a crimson cord, which is tied around the dragon's neck.[1]

The angel is the Divine Intellect or Spirit; the crown, the rational mind in obedience to the Spirit; St. George, the human will in

---

1. The crimson cord is associated with two prostitutes in the Old Testament: Tamar, daughter-in-law of Judah who disguised herself as a harlot after her husband died, lured Judah to sleep with her and became pregnant by him, because he had broken his promise to give her another one of his sons for a husband—when her son Zarah was born, the nurse tied a red cord around his hand [Gen. 38:6–30]—and Rahab, who hid the spies of Joshua at her house in Jericho before the Children of Israel laid siege to that city, and hung a red cord from her window during the siege as a sign for the victorious Israelites to spare her life [Joshua 2:1–22; 6:22–25]. To this day in Israel a red cord is wrapped around the tombstone of Rachel, then cut into lengths and distributed as a protective charm, called Rachel's Bracelet, to be wrapped seven times around the wrist. The word *Rachel* means 'sheep' or 'lamb' and is said to indicate humility and submission; Rachel is also associated with mother-hood and fertility in Judaism. According to the Kabbalists, Rachel's Bracelet sym-bolizes the struggle against the passional soul, the *nefesh*, a Hebrew word strictly synonymous with the Arabic *nafs*; this is undoubtedly also the significance of the red cord by which the Princess leads the dragon in the icon of St. George, who is associated in the Near East with Elijah as well as Khidr. And Tamar, strangely enough, is considered by Eastern Orthodox Christians to be a prefiguration of the Blessed Virgin, the Theotokos ('mother of God'). Without victory over the passions there is no spiritual fertility; for God to be born in our hearts, the dragon of the *nafs* must first be slain, then conquered, then pacified, then put to work.

obedience to the Spirit via the rational mind; the horse, those aspects of the *nafs* which have become submissive to the will, and thus ultimately to the Spiritual Intellect; the dragon, the as-yet-unredeemed aspects of the *nafs* as fallen Mercury, in the process of being fixed by St. George as redeemed Sulfur. That the dragon lies on a lake of solid (though not icy) water represents him as coagulating Mercury, which in its fallen aspect is lovelessness—the petrification of the affections—and in its redeemed aspect, emotional stability. The lance wielded by St. George is the *axis mundi*, which in terms of the soul represents the true hierarchy of the human faculties. This is the active, masculine aspect of the transmutation.

The feminine aspect—the goal of the transmutation already virtually present—is represented by the remaining figures. The princess is Mercury in its highest state, Mercury fixed as Silver, the redeemed human soul in which the three primal faculties of rationality, affect and will—the king, the queen and the prince—are in perfect balance on the psychic plane. This is the feminine, *horizontal* complement to their *vertical* hierarchicalization in which the masculine principle takes precedence. The tower is another representation of the soul, its vertical nature another symbol of the *axis mundi*, which the horizontal balance of the faculties can never replace, but must always complement. And the dragon which the princess holds by a leash is the unredeemed *nafs* as Sulfur, in the process of being tamed and redeemed by Love, by dissolving Mercury, the soul in its feminine essence. The very bond which began as a dominance of passion over Love, has now become—without the position of the two figures being changed in any way—a sovereignty of Love over passion.

When the soul is submitted to God, Sulfur and Mercury unite. Sulfur, now redeemed, becomes the rational mind, governing the will as vice-regent of the Intellect; Mercury is now the affections as submissive to the will, and therefore ultimately obedient to the same Intellect. In active terms, the feminine or affective principle occupies the lowers rung of the hierarchy; in receptive terms, however, She is Silver, the pole of pure Substance, the perfect Mirror of the Divine Intellect, a receptive perfection which the masculine principle, in its twin modes of will and rationality, can never attain.

The union of the masculine and feminine principles within the soul is in one sense simultaneous, since it happens in a realm transcending linear time. In another sense, however, it is successive. According to this point of view, Mercury must first 'solve' the willful prejudices and fixed ideas of Sulfur, melting the hardness of egotism and allowing all things to merge and flow, after which Sulfur can embrace and 'fix' with its hierarchical lance the elusive capriciousness of Mercury, so that the chaotic impulses of the soul—the subconscious counterpart of hardened egotism—are ordered and harmonized. The same story is told in hexagrams 31 and 32 of the *I Ching*. In 31, *Wooing*, the masculine principle places itself below the feminine; in 32, *Duration*, the hexagram for marriage, it stands above the feminine. So even though the masculine principle is hierarchically exalted over the feminine, the primal impulse to the redemption of the human soul emanates from the feminine pole, from that 'virginal' receptivity within us which says, in the words of the Virgin Mary, 'let it be done unto me according to Thy word.' This is why, in alchemy, the 'hermetic art', Mercury is both the effective potency which makes the Great Work possible, and the psychopomp who guides the worker through the various stages of it, and why, in the icon of St. George, the queen on the tower (the tower being also a traditional symbol of the Virgin) stands *between* the king and the prince: affection, when purified, mediates between rationality (the king, the father) and will (the prince, the son), and reconciles them. And when affection is fully submitted to will, as will is to the rational mind, then, as the lowest principle, it regains its primordial power to reflect the highest principle, higher even than the rational mind: the transcendent Intellect itself, in which Love and Knowledge are one.

# THE PRACTICE OF SALT

*For John Eberly*

*You are the salt of the earth—*
*but if the salt loses its saltiness,*
*what can it be salted with?*
Matt. 5:13

SULFUR is form, impulse. Mercury is material to be formed, and also the fuel or energy of impulse. Salt is the body, the matrix—the *athanor*, the *thalamos* ('wedding chamber')—the vessel in which they unite.

When we are internally divided, at war with ourselves, our Sulfur and Mercury are at odds. The impulse to impose form becomes either tyrannical and violent, or flaky and flighty; the potential to receive form becomes either elusive and 'mercurial', or else sullen, in-turned and withdrawn; it either flees form or refuses to receive it. Consequently we are in a state of willfulness and moodiness, mania and depression—either that or petrification and flightiness, sulkiness and chaos. The more sulky or capricious Mercury becomes, the more violent becomes Sulfur's impulse to move it, its obsession to impose fixed form upon it—which, when it fails (as it must), turns into an explosive, dissipated impulse to totally express all possible forms. And the violence and inflexibility of Sulfur only make Mercury that much more mercurial, that much more deeply wounded and congealed. In the words of William Blake:

> *My Spectre around me night & day*
> *Like a Wild beast guards my way*
> *My Emanation far within*
> *Weeps incessantly for my Sin*

King and Queen, Sulfur and Mercury go to war with each other when there is not enough Salt in the mix. Salt is the body, but it is also the character. It is wisdom, lore, informing context, character-strength. It is flexibility, reliability, humility—even humor, and certainly courtesy. But it is also more than that. It is *tradition*, an integrated vessel composed of doctrinal and ritual forms; it is also *attention*, both as supported by those forms and as an act in itself. It transcends all polarities. It is their field, their context; it contains them; it is also beyond them. As the lowest is the signature of the highest, so Salt as 'body' is the signature of the unknowable Divine Essence. In the words of Jesus, 'none has seen the Father at any time,' and 'who has seen me has seen the Father.'

Salt is that which witnesses the polarity of Sulfur and Mercury without becoming involved with it. The divided soul is always identifying itself with its willfulness or its passiveness, its violent obsessiveness or its desire to hide and sleep. Sometimes it identifies with Sulfur, sometimes with Mercury—and whenever it identifies with one of the pair consciously, it always identifies with the other unconsciously.

Salt, however, is beyond identification. In its higher sense, as the 'body' of the marriage of Sulfur and Mercury, it is formless, substanceless, neither agent nor patient. It is pure Witness, the vessel and seed of Gold. So the practice of Salt is: to witness Sulfur and Mercury—*forma* and *materia*, impulse and *potentia*, active will and stored-up power—without fleeing, and without interfering. The identification of consciousness with its active and passive modes is what hides them from each other, prevents them from relating fruitfully with each other, and sets them at war. Salt breaks this identification. When Salt is added, Sulfur and Mercury become mutually aware; they balance each other, embrace each other. There is no conscious attempt to force them together (that would be Sulfur alone), nor any more aimless drifting in the currents of identification and desire (that would be Mercury alone); there is only the conscious withdrawal of the unconscious ego identification that has for so long held them apart. To sit still, to witness *deliberately*, and not to interfere—that takes real Salt.

# IV

## SUFISM AND ITS FRIENDS

*Excursions in*
*Esoteric Ecumenism*

This house of safety, this secret cell, this hidden
    chamber of pleasure
Where best friends meet—
Whoever has found his way into our company
Has found the locked and guarded house
Where a hundred doors stand open.

[*after Hafiz*]

# CHRISTIAN & MUSLIM 'TRINITARIANISM'

## *A Reply to Philip Sherrard*

Eastern Orthodox Christian writer Philip Sherrard has sometimes been identified as a member of the so-called 'Traditionalist' school, founded by René Guénon and brought to profound fruition by Frithjof Schuon. And yet in his last book, *Christianity: The Lineaments of a Sacred Tradition*, in the final chapter entitled 'The Logic of Metaphysics'—though certainly not in the greater part of the book— he seems on the verge of breaking with them over the fundamental doctrine of the Impersonal Absolute, which Guénon most often understands in terms of the Vedanta, but which is to be found in every sacred tradition, including Christianity. Certainly an idolatry of the Formless Absolute as a mental concept, often with the motive of avoiding both the efficacious warmth of devotion to God and all generosity and compassion in our relations with our fellow human beings, is a besetting sin of many attracted to the study of metaphysics. And the cold, mathematical precision of Guénon's writings reveals a personality which, while proper to his specific mission, should clearly not be taken as a model for most believers, or even most mystics, Muslim or otherwise. One wonders if Sherrard, in the face of the recent turbulence in the Traditionalist world, and under the shadow of his own impending death, may have mistaken the *sang froid* of a French metaphysical intellectual for the supposed heartlessness of the 'desert' of the Godhead, the Formless Absolute.

But such speculations as to Sherrard's motives are in a way unfair. His opposition to the idea of a Formless Absolute was undoubtedly sincere, and based on specific metaphysical objections to Guénon's position. It is these objections alone that I will essay to answer; as we Muslims say, 'may God keep his secret.'

## I. VARIETY AND PARADOX IN
## CHRISTIAN THEISTIC AND TRINITARIAN LANGUAGE

Metaphysical discourse must walk a fine line between a total dedication to Truth and a realization that all metaphysical statements are
'operative' in a sense, ultimately justified only by the effect they produce on our consciousness. A statement that is 'true' but does not
*convey* Truth in no way serves the goal of metaphysics, which is to
prepare the heart not to resist, through an attachment to error, the
direct intuition of Divine realities. This is why the Buddha considered such questions as whether or not human consciousness survives bodily death, or whether the Tathagata does or does not exist
after attaining Nirvana, as 'tending not to edification'. To the Buddhists, doctrine is an aspect of *upaya* or operative method. If it
breaks our attachment to erroneous ideas, it is true; if not, then not.
On the other hand, the clear, objective and orthodox expression of
Divine Truth, even though it is incapable of totally encompassing
the Truth it expresses, is one of the most powerful of *upayas*, which is
why the Buddhists, even while repudiating metaphysics (as the
Theravadins and the Zen practitioners do) also produced metaphysical systems of great subtlety and complexity (as, for example, that of
the Vajrayana school, or the Madhyamika). To idolize metaphysical
formulations as if they were absolutely true, rather than 'quasi-abso-
lutely' necessary within a given context, is to miss the Truth by the
positive road, which is literalism; to take such formulations as mere
utilitarian tools for the manipulation of consciousness is to miss it
by the negative road, which is nihilism. Apophatic mysticism is the
remedy for the first disease, cataphatic mysticism for the second.

This reciprocal relationship between metaphysical speech and
metaphysical silence can be applied to Christian doctrine as well.
Thus when Christians say that God is personal, they are indicating
that everything we know as personhood is derived from Him, Who
is nonetheless greater than any sense of personhood we can conceive
of. Insofar as Eastern Orthodox theology denies the precedence of
an impersonal Absolute over the persons of the Trinity—if it really
does—this is to prevent Christians from forming a false image of
an abstract, impersonal 'beyond-being' in the face of which God's

personhood dwindles to 'mere' personality. But then the nearly universal testimony of the Christian mystics arises—including that pillar of Eastern Orthodoxy, Dionysius the Areopagite, in his *Mystical
Theology*—who tell us of a 'Godhead', a 'dazzling obscurity', a 'Divine
desert' in which no forms can be discerned, including those of the
Trinity, over which, in the mystical *extasis*, it is seen to take precedence, while in no way negating or subordinating this Trinity.

How can the Godhead take precedence over the Trinity without
subordinating it? If we place logic above intellection, there is no way
it can. If, however, we give intellection precedence over logic, then
the problem simply disappears. If the doctrine of the absolute unity
of the Divine Essence with its trinitarian embodiment protects the
Christian sense of the Absolute from an abstract impersonalism, the
testimony of the apophatic mystics to the transpersonal Godhead
equally protects the sense of God's Personhood from a literalistic
and anthropomorphic belief, leading to a sentimental personalism
fundamentally indistinguishable from polytheism, that the Divine
Persons can somehow be encompassed by human understanding—
as well as guarding in its own way the notion of God's Essence
against a lapse into the abstract and impersonal, since it is into this
very Essence, an Essence which is both their original Source and
their ultimate Reality, that the Persons are subsumed in the apophatic ecstasy.

The sense of the Trinity as a possible object of knowledge is
essential to the purity and efficacy of Christian doctrine. And yet, in a
truer sense, the Trinity cannot be an object of *our* knowledge, since it
is precisely the necessary mode of God's knowledge of, and love of,
Himself. In one sense the Son is the *form* of the Father's self-
knowledge and self-love in eternity, while the Holy Spirit is the *act* of
that self-knowledge and self-love. In another sense, the Son, from the
Christian perspective, is Jesus Christ, the unique incarnation of God's
eternal self-knowledge and self-love in space and time. But in a third
sense—which cannot be separated from the other two without
lapsing into heresy from a Christian standpoint—the Son is precisely
the human being *in Divinis,* as when St. Paul says 'it is not I who live,
but Christ lives in me,' or Jesus answers the accusation of Pharisees
that he claims divinity for himself by saying 'do not the scriptures

teach that ye are all gods and sons of the Most High?' The Second Person of the Trinity would thus be analogous to the Sufi concept of *al-Insan al-Kamil*, the Perfect Man, which is both the archetype of humanity *in Divinis* and site of manifestation of all the Most Beautiful Names, and the perfection of the human being who has realized his or her archetype. In this sense, the Trinity is precisely the relationship between man and God which pertains after man has attained *theosis*. If God became man that man might become God, then the Son is none other than the Christ *in me*. The Father is the God Whom, even though by Christ's power I have attained Godhood, I worship as greater than myself, as when Jesus said 'why do you call me good? None is good but the Father.' And the Holy Spirit is the essential Love and Knowledge Who unites the Christ in me with the Father Who is eternally above me; one might almost say that, after *theosis*, (and, virtually, even beforehand), the Son is myself as a son of God and co-heir with Christ; the Father, the Unseen God Whom I acknowledge as having precedence over me in terms of 'procession', though He and I are of one Essence; and the Holy Spirit, the very Unity of Father and Son. Yet 'it is not I who live, but Christ lives in me.' In my created humanity I am in no way God. Deification or *theosis* is not the perfection of myself as creature—to claim such perfection would be to rival God—but the realized perfection of the Divine within me, by virtue of the Second Person of the Trinity, the archetype of my Humanity, 'made in the image and likeness of God.' When Jesus said 'be ye perfect as your Heavenly Father is perfect,' he was not requiring that 'flesh' make itself equal to 'Spirit', but rather, through the Son Who lives in the center and depth of the soul, that the perfection of the Father be realized, since 'I and the Father are one.'[2]

The fullness of the Godhead is present in all three Persons—and yet there is still a precedence between them. If this were not so, Eastern Orthodox theology would not insist so strongly that the Holy

2. The irreducible theological barrier between Christianity and Islam, even Sufic Islam, appears to be the *exclusive uniqueness* of Jesus as representative of the Human Archetype *in Divinis*, in light of Muhammad's statement that 'I make no distinction between the prophets (Jesus being considered a great prophet in Islam), though the statement of Jesus that 'ye are all gods and sons of the Most High' would

Spirit proceeds not from the Father *and* the Son, as in Catholic theology, but from the Father alone. The Father takes precedence, as a hypostasis of the Formless Absolute, the Divine Essence as It is in Itself, over both the Son and the Spirit. And yet the fullness of this Divine Essence is equally present in all three Persons. The Spirit is the infinite radiance of the Father; consequently, in the Orthodox formulation of the Trinity, He would be related to Guénon's (and Schuon's) Infinite, as the Father is to Schuon's Absolute. And if the Spirit is Infinite Possibility, then the Son is Perfection (Schuon's third divine 'hypostasis' along with Absoluteness and Infinity), the perfect synthesis of those Infinite Possibilities, and thus the perfect mirror, or image, or *icon* of the unknowable Father, as when Jesus says both 'none have seen the Father at any time' and 'who has seen me has seen the Father.' Seen from the standpoint of God's Self-manifestation, the Father or Formless Absolute must come 'first', (though first neither in time nor in Essence); the Holy Spirit, as the radiance of this Absolute in terms of Infinite Possibility, and the 'only-begotten' Son, as the Father's perfect self-expression, 'without whom nothing that is made was made' (since all manifest existence is necessarily derived from the form of God's eternal self-knowledge), must yield precedence—in terms of manifestation, not Essence—to the Father. This is why Eastern Orthodox theology defines the second and third Persons of the Trinity as 'proceeding from the Father'. Nonetheless, in terms of redemption rather than creation, the Catholic formulation of trinitarian doctrine, in which the Holy Spirit proceeds from the Father *and* the Son, is also true, since even though the Holy Spirit is sent by the Father, this Spirit cannot be hypostasized as a distinct Person without the relationship

---

seem to deny this literal exclusivity. In my opinion, only Frithjof Schuon's doctrine of the transcendent unity of religions can resolve this dichotomy—though not in the world of form. God blesses each unique and spiritually-operative perspective He has established for our salvation—that is, each religious revelation—with His Own Absoluteness, thus rendering each of them, in Schuon's terminology, 'relatively Absolute'. Each, from its own perspective, is the Absolute Itself. These 'perspectives' are not subjective, however; they are not based upon belief: they are as objective as seven different trails up the slopes of Mt. Qaf, all headed for the One Summit.

*in Divinis* between Father and Son, Divine Source and Divine Manifestation, any more than this Spirit can manifest in human life
without the *relationship* between God-in-man ('It is not I who live,
but Christ lives in me') and the unseen Father—without God's
grace and the human response to it—without prayer. In Christian
terms, prayer is the communion of the Son within me with the
Father above me; in a certain sense, prayer itself *is* the Holy Spirit.
But this in no way makes the Spirit dependent for Its deployment
upon the attitude of a mere creature, since the relationship between
the unseen Father and Christ the Divine Man subsists in eternity,
before the foundation of the world. In Catholic formulation, then,
the Father is the Formless Absolute in the mode of polarity with Its
own manifestation *in divinis*—this relationship being a distinct Person, the Holy Spirit—while in the Eastern Orthodox formulation,
the Father is this same Absolute as It is in Itself, paradoxically
beyond all relations while at the same time being the Source of all
relations—the Source of all relations precisely *because* It is beyond
all relations.

## II. SOME SPECIFIC POINTS IN 'THE LOGIC OF METAPHYSICS' ANSWERED

(1) In his chapter 'The Logic of Metaphysics', Philip Sherrard
maintains that, according to Guénon, the Absolute is beyond logic
yet can be 'typified' by logic. This logic is Aristotelian and 'exclusionary': A cannot be both B and not-B. Sherrard faults Guénon for
applying exclusionary logic to the Absolute. But then,

(2) He does the same thing himself when he criticizes Guénon's
formulation that 'Being is determined by nothing; it determines
itself.' In trying to catch Guénon in a logical contradiction, he is
himself applying exclusionary logic to the Absolute, thereby falling
into the same error he attributes to Guénon. An undetermined
which determines itself is a logical contradiction, true; but the fact is
that logic does not apply on the level of the question 'how can a
totally undetermined non-dual Absolute generate duality and determination?' Only paradoxical language can be applied to this 'mystery', which, as *maya*, will always escape a strictly logical definition.

(3) Sherrard understands that a purely negative description of the Absolute as non-determined (non-constrained) contains a subtle determination (constraint): the constraint of the Absolute that would seem to prevent it from generating determinations/constraints. Ibn al-'Arabi has dealt conclusively with this point, in his doctrine that 'the Absolute is not delimited by its own non-delimitation.' But then,

(4) Sherrard deals with this apparent contradiction by saying that the Absolute and the non-manifest divine Essence should not (as in Guénon) be identified, and does so using what he calls a 'radical' apophatic language, according to which neither positive nor negative language can be applied to the Absolute. But he makes the error of placing Being and Not-Being on the same ontological level as the two sides of a horizontal paradox, whereas the truth is that Non-Being is higher than Being, and the identity of Being and Not-Being higher still. Thus he says 'If the Absolute is free from determination, it is also not free from determination,' whereas it is more accurate to say that 'If the Absolute is free from determination, it is also free from non-determination'; an Absolute which is 'not free from determination' is in no way Absolute. In Buddhist terms, the realization of Nirvana liberates us from Sangsara, while the realization of the identity of Sangsara and Nirvana liberates us from a reified and subtly conceptual Nirvana. Likewise Being is the truth which liberates us from contingency (religious faith saves us from the world); Not-Being, that which liberates us from an attachment to Being (apophatic mysticism overcomes the subtle self-worship inherent in our worship of God on the plane of form); and the understanding of the Absolute as transcending both Being and Not-Being, that which liberates us from a one-sided mystical transcendentalism (the origin of heretical Gnosticism) which denies that the Absolute is capable of encompassing and manifesting Itself as the contingent and determined without losing its absoluteness (plenary esoterism overcomes the excesses and imbalances of apophatic mysticism). So Sherrard is right in saying that the Absolute transcends even Essence, if we take Essence as excluding all determination, but he is clearly wrong in denying that Essence is higher than determination, and asserting that it is simply the other side of the polarity

'Unmanifest Essence/Manifest Determinations'. To put it succinctly, the ultimate identity of Being and Not-Being can be realized only through Not-Being, not through Being, though subsequent to this realization it is certainly *manifest* through Being. And if we identify 'Not-Being' with 'Beyond-Being', as Guénon did, then we can't take it as simply the horizontal opposite term to 'Being', but must understand it as ultimately qualifiable neither by 'Being' nor by 'Non-Being', and thus as identical with Sherrard's 'Absolute'.

(5) Sherrard, somewhat puzzlingly, faults Guénon for being a 'pantheist' because his doctrine implicitly denies the reality of manifestation. But is not pantheism the doctrine according to which manifestation is mistaken for its Principle, and thus taken as a kind of a spurious absolute? One would have thought that accusations of Gnosticism or Manichaeism would have come more readily to Sherrard's mind—though Guénon is no more a Gnostic (in the sectarian, heretical sense) than he is a pantheist. Furthermore, when Sherrard places Being and Not-Being on the same ontological level as aspects of the one Absolute, without hierarchicalizing them, he is more of a pantheist than Guénon is.

(6) Like many today, Sherrard can only see a flat contradiction between the values of the particular and personal and the spectre of the Non-dual Absolute. He seems to believe, in Chestertonian mode, that the personal is somehow horribly negated in this Absolute, as if the Godhead of the mystics were a desecration of all that is good and genuine in human life, a kind of total alienation. The Non-dual Absolute, however—*Nirguna Brahman*—is not so much impersonal as *Transpersonal*—otherwise the personal God could not be Its first intelligible manifestation. Likewise the personal God—*Saguna Brahman*—is not limited by His personhood, but 'open within' to the Transpersonal (as, in fact, all persons are, who otherwise would be nothing but limited and predictable sets of physical and psychic characteristics: caricatures, not characters). In the words of Ramana Maharshi, '*bhakti* is the love of God with form' (*Saguna Brahman*); '*jñana* is the love of God without form' (*Nirguna Brahman*)—and where there is an 'impersonality' which negates personhood rather than transcending it, there can obviously be no love. Love requires Person as its object; it equally requires the

Transpersonal dimension, which is all that prevents the Person of God—or of one's human beloved—from being treated as a known and defined quantity, reified, and consequently imprisoned within the shell of one's ego, rendering the loved one drearily predictable, all-too-well known.

## III. TRINITARIANISM IN ISLAMIC METAPHYSICS

According to the Islamic testimony of faith, 'there is no god but God.' Exoterically, this means there is only one Supreme Being; eso-terically, this indicates that there is only one Being; God alone pos-sesses the attribute of Being, along with all other attributes; you and I are nothing in ourselves—yet we appear, we act, we love, we suffer, God sends us prophets and Books to save us, and we have the power to submit to His Will—though not, paradoxically, unless He Him-self wills it. So who are we? We are none other than Him (who else could we be, there being none else?), but only insofar as we attribute no Being to ourselves, and all to Him. (To attribute this Being to 'ourselves and all things' rather than to Him would be the error of pantheism.) The responsibility to submit is ours; the command to submit, and thus the reality of submission, is His. If we were to pos-sess being and essence of our own to place beside His Being and Essence (this being the sin of *shirk*, analogous to the Christian 'sin against the Holy Ghost'), then God would be a capricious tyrant, a personification of fate or literalistic predestination, since He would either submit or not submit *for* me, dooming me to Paradise or the Fire without action or obedience on my part. But since my Essence is none other than His, His Essence does not stand, will, or exist apart from or over against mine; He in no way limits my choice; I am free with His freedom to participate either in the eternal Mercy or the eternal Wrath of His Nature, according to the name of God I am from all eternity, a name both freely chosen (since there is no Being in me but God's Being, and God is free) and eternally des-tined (since God is Who He is, and cannot be otherwise).

From the point-of-view of exoteric Islam, trinitarianism is seen as tri-theism. This is obviously a misunderstanding of Christian doctrine, yet it is accurate to one of the ways Christian doctrine can degenerate or be misunderstood—like the view of the iconoclasts that icons are intrinsically idols. In essence they are not idols, otherwise any sensible or even intelligible 'sign' of God would be so too, including the Holy Qur'an; just as certainly, in common with all sensible or intelligible forms, they can be transformed into idols through ego-identification.

From the Muslim standpoint, to say 'Trinity transcends Unity' is an error, as I believe it also is from the Christian standpoint. 'The single nature of the Three is God' says St. Gregory Nazianzen. 'In regard to His oneness he is the Father. The others come from Him and return to Him without being confused with one another. They coexist with Him, without being separated in time, in purpose, or in power.' If the single nature of the Trinity is God, Who in regard to His oneness is identified with the Father, then Trinity cannot transcend Unity, but is rather the eternal expression of Unity.

Sufi metaphysics, as I understand it, would include the doctrine that trinity is the necessary manifestation of Unity according to the form of the act of cognition (mine, and God's too; it is not exclusively subjective, or exclusively cosmic), and thus that it is—as in Schuon's *maya-in-divinis*—necessarily virtual within Unity; to affirm the Unity of God is to *participate* in trinity. Certainly if 'the Unity of God's Essence' is seen as a mere abstract 'Godness' which must *logically* be possessed by the three Persons, since all three are God, then it no way transcends these Persons. They are concrete; it is a mere abstraction from that concreteness. But that's not what— or Who—the Unity of God's Essence is. By 'essence', here, I do not mean 'quiddity', the Islamic *mahiyya*, but the Absolute Essence, the Islamic *Dhat*. *Mahiyya* relates to the question 'what is it?' and must be answered by comparing the object in question to other objects: X is what it is because it is like A and not like B, etc. God certainly transcends *mahiyya*; God is not this or that object. *Dhat*, on the other hand, as Absolute Essence, is incomparable; It is incapable of being defined in terms other than Itself. When God said to Moses, 'I Am That I Am,' he was speaking out of that Incomparable Essence, identified with pure Being—which, we must remember, is in another sense superessential and Beyond Being.

Islam also has a doctrine of God as Being and Beyond Being.

Being is *Allah;* Beyond Being, the Divine Essence, is *Dhat* or *Hu.* In one way, *Allah* is the Personal God Whom Schuon identifies with pure Being. Yet the word *Allah* literally means 'The Deity'—an impersonal name—while the designation for the 'impersonal' Essence or Beyond Being is *Hu,* which means 'He'—a personal name. The many names of God are names of the Essence; their totality and synthesis is *Allah.* In one sense they are qualities, attributes, and thus relatively abstract vis-à-vis the Essence; in another sense they are precisely *names* which, like all names, denote the essence of someone insofar as it transcends that someone's definable attributes. This is one of the ways the paradoxical *dance* (cf. the Christian *perichoresis*) of the Impersonal/Personal Transpersonal God is rendered in Sufi metaphysics.

The fundamental Muslim testimony of faith is 'there is no god but God'—and if I, through my essential nothingness, am His slave *(abd),* and thereby his fully-empowered representative in this world *(khalifa),* and thus (finally) His symbol, whose archetype is the Perfect Man, *al-Insan al-Kamil,* God's first intelligible act of Self-understanding from all eternity (according to Ibn al-'Arabi, al-Jili and al-Iraqi)—He who *is* the cosmos *in divinis,* just as I, as man, am the compendium of the cosmos in creation; and if I (as servant), Allah (as Lord, a Name which can only be applied to Him if a servant exists whose Lord He can be), and the Divine Reality which unites us, share the one and only Being and Essence, which is God's, then this is precisely the esoteric trinitarianism within Islam (or one of several versions of it), in which the trinity is not, however, an intelligible and revealed Divine Object, with myself as the subject viewing it, but is precisely God's act of Self-understanding within me, and *as* me. From this point of view, possible in terms of esoteric Islam, and perhaps not fundamentally opposed to Christian trinitarianism, though necessarily possessing a different nuance and probably lacking true spiritual efficacy in a Christian context, the trinity is not a the 'literal' nature of a God Who, in reality, is in every sense other than me, being One without a second; rather, the act of intellection—which in the inner sense is God's eternal act of Self-understanding, inseparable from His Nature, and in the outer sense both the creation of the cosmos from God and its reintegration in

God—is itself trinitarian. The act of intellection *in Divinis* is the archetype of the Divine act of creation. According to Ibn al-'Arabi, the Divine Essence in Its eternal manifestation polarizes into Creator and cosmos, which in Essence are none other than the Reality, in which their polarity is eternally resolved. The Essence of Lord, Servant and Reality, or of Creator, Cosmos and Reality, is none other than God's Essence. Yet, in terms of form, I remain God's servant, just as the cosmos remains God's creation; both servant and cosmos are totally contingent upon Him alone. (See the *Fusus al-Hikam*, the chapter 'Salih'.)

So at the serious risk of mixing doctrines proper to different traditions in the wrong way, I am compelled to declare that Meister Eckhart's formulation 'The eye through which God sees me and the eye through which I see Him are the same eye'—Eckhart who truly was the 'Christian Ibn al-'Arabi' if I may so express it—defines a trinitarianism which I, as a Muslim and dervish who holds to the metaphysics of Ibn al-'Arabi, can fully accept:

'The eye through which God sees me' (the Father Whom 'none has seen at any time'; the Divine Essence in the sense of the Unwitnessed Witness, the Vedantic *Atman)* 'and the eye through which I see God' (the Son; the site-of-manifestation of the Divine Essence; the primordial human nature, *al-fitrah,* as expressed in the *hadith* 'heaven and earth cannot contain Me, but the heart of my loving slave can contain Me', and in words of Jesus, 'who has seen me has seen the Father') 'are the same eye' (the Holy Spirit; the Universality of God; the Unity of Father and Son in the Absolute Reality). In Ibn al-'Arabi's terms, 'I' am the Servant, 'God' is the Lord, our common 'Eye' is the Reality.

## IV. THE TRINITARIANISM OF FRITHJOF SCHUON

In my opinion, all that Christian theology can (and should) nail down in terms of trinitarian dogma is that the Deity is One God in Three Divine Persons. The dispute—which Bishop Kallistos Ware, for one, de-emphasizes—between the Catholic formulation where the Holy Spirit proceeds from the Father and the Son—the famous, thorny *filioque* —and the Orthodox formulation, where the Spirit proceeds from the Father alone, is simply one of perspective. As I indicated above, the Orthodox formulation apparently sees the Holy Spirit as the creative and saving radiance of the Father, which comes to man through the Son, whereas the Catholic formulation sees the Holy Spirit more as the relationship between Father and Son, as in prayer.

The Traditionalist diagram can be helpful here. In general, the Traditionalists tend to speak schematically of the Father as the midpoint of the circle, the Holy Spirit as the radii, and the Son as the circumference. Insofar as the radii radiate from the Center, the Holy Spirit proceeds from the Father. Insofar as a 'radius' is precisely a straight line which unites Center and Circumference, the Holy Spirit proceeds from both Father and Son. The Father is the Source of the Spirit; but if there were no Son, there would be no recipient of that Spirit, which would never become intelligible, never be deployed as a distinct hypostasis; consequently the name 'Holy Spirit' could never be known.

The Church Fathers themselves speak of the Trinity from many different perspectives. The Father is the oneness of God, or else the engendering force within the Divine Nature. The Son is the creative ray of the Father, yet everything God does is done by the Spirit. The Son is the perfection of all things, yet the Holy Spirit is the one who brings all to perfection. What I see in this apparent mass of contradictions is the truth, which Schuon expresses so well, that metaphysics is suggestive, not dogmatic; it must speak from a multitude of perspectives, since by nature it is attempting to express, or give intuitions of, something which cannot and should not be made explicit. It can and should be expressed in terms of logic, insofar as is possible—and such expression is far more possible than is generally believed—but it cannot be trapped in logic. Theology is the necessary vessel of metaphysics; the metaphysical multiplicity of perspectives is no excuse for heterodoxy; it doesn't mean that you can say anything you want to; it is not subjective or impressionistic; some formulations are simply wrong. But if the Church Fathers can present many different versions of the Trinity in their attempt to render that mystery—versions which as theology would be contradictory, but which as metaphysics are precisely paradoxical—then perhaps the trinitarianism of Frithjof Schuon, based on the three hypostases the Absolute, the Infinite and the Perfect, and which is also situated on the plane of metaphysics, not that of theology, is no less orthodox.

The Absolute, the Infinite and the Perfect, for Schuon, are three and not three. Infinity is not Infinity in isolation, but precisely the Infinity of the Absolute, which is not other than Perfection. Neither is Absoluteness isolated in its own nature, being the essence of both Infinity and Perfection. Nor can Perfection be separated from either the Absolute or the Infinite, since it is the site of their manifestation and the Vessel of their Union. These three hypostases are expressed in impersonal terms, yet in Schuon's doctrine they also have a personal aspect. Absoluteness, the principle of transcendence and thereby hierarchy, is the archetype of everything masculine. Infinity, the principle of immanence and thereby all-embracing and all-constituting Substance, is the archetype of everything feminine. And Perfection is the archetype of Divine Form, in which all manifestation, as well as manifestation's unseen Source, are gathered into perfect synthesis, *al-Insan-al-Kamil* or Perfect Man, the secret of God's eternal self-knowledge in the depths of His nature, which is the prototype *in Divinis* of the human form. Certainly this is not Christian theology any more than it is Muslim *kalam,* nor is it meant to replace them. Its specific function is to protect the providential and necessary formulations of theology from petrifying into idols, and also to point beyond them, directly to the Object of which they are the signposts here in this world. It is, precisely, metaphysics, which as Schuon points out is as much 'musical' as 'mathematical'. It is the dance of the human mind on the shores of the Inexpressible. It is the reflection of what the eternal Essence that expressed itself on earth as Philip Sherrard is gazing upon, God willing, even now. As death is swallowed up in victory, so hearsay, and even sight itself, are swallowed up in the taste, and the embrace.

# EXCERPT FROM A LETTER
# TO A CHRISTIAN MYSTIC
# FROM PORTUGAL

IT WAS NOT for nothing that the Virgin Mary appeared in a town in your homeland named after Fatima, the daughter of the Prophet Muhammad (peace and blessings be upon him)—Fatima who in Muslim veneration is second only to Mary, and who, if it had not been for Mary herself, would have been the closest thing to her equivalent in the Islamic tradition. In Shi'ism she has almost become a Queen of Heaven in her own right. And as Mary is slighted in certain places in the Gospels—'woman, what have I to do with thee?'—so Fatima was seemingly treated unfairly by her father the Prophet, who did not let her inherit the Fadak Oasis, and perhaps also by the first Caliph, Abu Bakr, whose election by the community over her husband Ali (whom the Shi'ites and the Sufis consider to be the Prophet's spiritual heir) placed her in a difficult position. And then, like Mary, in later years Fatima became exalted to near-divine status. All this, in my opinion, has something to do with mystery of the feminine reflection of Divinity, which is a secret that must be kept until the dawning of the Hour. Look at all the problems, from the Gnostics to Soloviev, which grew out of attempts to make 'sophianic' spirituality explicit within Christianity. Where is Mary as *hypostasis* to be placed? As a fourth person of the Trinity? And yet there is a mystery in her which is incomparably exalted—the mystery of perfect *islam*, of the pure, self-annihilating receptivity-to-God of the perfected soul, which thereby becomes host to the Divinity. As the Sufis say, the soul does not become God, but is annihilated in His presence; then there is only He. But when there is only He, then there is nothing that does not reflect Him or participate in His nature, and so the soul paradoxically remains—

annihilated in its separateness but remaining forever as a pure gift, to nothingness, of God's own Being. And so, in a certain sense, all things are names of God. I am in no way God—but God *is* most certainly me. I am nothing but His veil; He is entirely my Being.

The veil, the *hijab*, imposed (intermittently) upon women after the Prophet's time, can certainly be an abuse. Yet there is a secret in the feminine nature which must be kept at all cost. Mary is the deepest secret of creation; when this secret is finally told in its completeness, then the Hour will come. That's when the veil of the Temple will be torn in two—not just in the inner chamber, but for the whole world.

The equivalent of Mary in Islam is the Prophet Muhammad; his receptivity to the Qur'an is compared to Mary's receptivity to the Holy Spirit. As in Christianity the Word is made flesh, so in Islam the Word is made book—and both advents were announced by the angel Gabriel. The coming of the Word of God in Christianity is an Incarnation, and in Islam a Theophany. When the Eucharist is received, it becomes part of the living body of the recipient. When the words of the Qur'an are recited, they strike like lightning on a dark night. And then go out. And then come again. In the same way, God, by his Word, creates and re-creates the world in every instant.

Muslims usually consider the Christian Trinity to be a kind of tritheism, which is a misunderstanding of Christian theology, but a very accurate critique of Christian idolatry.

When the Qur'an says 'He neither begets nor is begotten, and there is nothing to which He can be compared,' it announces the Divine Transcendence in tones easily found in Christianity as well; the *Mystical Theology* of Dionysius the Areopagite comes immediately to mind. And passages in the Gospels such as 'why do you call me good? There is no-one is good but one, that is, God' are not lost on Muslims. When the Qur'an speaks of Jesus as *a Word of God and a Spirit from Him*, what is being asserted is simply that God cannot beget a second God like Himself, as a human father can beget a son who, in turn, can also become a father. When Eastern Orthodox theologians assert that Christ proceeds from the Father, not the other way around—which is why the Father is called Father—they are saying that the Father is Origin and the Son is second in procession;

he is a Word spoken and (by the Holy Spirit) a Spirit proceeding from the Father. (When Catholic theology asserts that the Holy Spirit proceeds from the Father *and* the Son, this simply means that, without the Son, there would be no 'point of destination' for the outflow of the Spirit, Who would therefore never be deployed as a distinct hypostasis.)

So Christ is a Word of God and a Spirit (breath) proceeding from Him, not a separate or second God. When we speak a word, that word reveals us; it does not become us. Yet Christian theology asserts that the Son is equal in divinity to the Father, for all that he emptied Himself and took on the form of a servant. Christ is a Word of God, not a second God….and yet when that Word is spoken in eternity, when It is co-eternal with the Speaker….what then? Islam will never accept the literal divinity of Jesus; yet in Sufi metaphysics, notably that of Ibn al-'Arabi of Andalusia—who felt himself to be under the special tutelage of the Prophet Jesus—Being can legitimately be attributed, as an intrinsic essence, only to God; all other things exist as gifts freely given by that One Being to nothingness, since everything that is apart from Him, in its own essence, can only be nothingness. So even though nothing that can be attributed to me as a creature is or can ever become God, nonetheless my Being and Essence are God Himself, and nothing else. 'Ye are all gods, and sons of the Most High'—not in our separate forms, which can no more attain to or be united with God than a flashlight can shine its light on the sun, but in our essence, which is already and only Him. If there is no God but God, as in the Muslim testimony of faith, then there is no Being but the One Being; this is the essence of the Sufi message.

As for its denial of the Crucifixion, the Qur'an does so partly in line with its conception that every prophet sent by God is virtually perfect—a far cry from the Old Testament view of Moses, for example, or Jonah, or King David, all three of whom are considered prophets in Islam. (This sense of the perfection of every prophet, though they differ in mission, capacity and degree of 'success', some of them having been martyred by the people to whom they were sent, gives the Muslim conception of Jesus as among the greatest of the prophets a nuance not transmitted simply by saying 'Muslims deny the divinity of Christ.') The Qur'an is saying that the Jews were not able to degrade or destroy God's prophet Jesus—for did he not walk free of all their schemes? This, of course, can never be reconciled with the doctrine of the Crucifixion and the Resurrection (though Martin Lings apparently saw the formulation 'Jesus was crucified in his humanity but not in His divinity' as a reconciliation of Christian and Muslim doctrine). But if God did indeed send Muhammad, peace and blessings be upon him, then He could not have sent Him with a doctrine identical to that of Christianity; if the Prophet had preached such a doctrine he would have been a Christian, and in no way a law-giving prophet (*rasul*) sent by God, which precisely is what he was. As it says in many places in the Qur'an, in the next world *Allah will enlighten them as to wherein they differ.*

# CREATION IS LOVE

## *With a Sufi Exegesis of a Traditional Catholic Prayer*

YOU WILL NEVER receive the love destined for you, or give the love you are destined to give, if you fail to realize the love you *are*.

You are a pure gift. At every breath you draw, your existence is breathed into you. It is Love; it is from Love. Love creates you, and Love is the substance of you. The pain of life hides this truth from you, but it is nonetheless true—truer than all the loss, truer than all the suffering. Existence itself—your own very existence—is pure Mercy.

This truth is expressed in the following traditional Catholic prayer (drawn mostly from the Psalms):

> *Come, Holy Spirit*
> *Fill the hearts of Thy faithful*
> *And enkindle in them the fire of Thy love.*
> *Send forth Thy Spirit and they shall be created,*
> *And Thou shalt renew the face of the earth.*

According to Ibn al-'Arabi's account of the creation, the permanent archetypes, all the possibilities of existence that rest eternally in God, the *ayan al-thabita*, longed for true existence, and God granted their wish. He breathed upon them the *Nafas al-Rahman*, the Breath of the Merciful, which brought them out of virtual existence into real existence.

The Holy Spirit is the *Nafas al-Rahman*, the Breath of Life. As this Breath is drawn into the soul, it creates that soul; it kindles the fire of the Heart, a gift of Being from the very Being of God. The Love of God which is the Breath of Life *creates* the faithful who receive it. In being created they are also redeemed—redeemed from the evil of non-entity.

If we long to be annihilated in God, then we must allow ourselves to be created. This is how the face of the earth, the face of earthly human existence, is renewed. If annihilation is the precondition of subsistence, creation is also the precondition of annihilation. Those who hold on to the illusion of self-creation are rejecting God's gift of His own Being; they are resisting His intent to bring them into the fullness of the human form. Before they were created they were only virtually human; now they are truly so. Before they had only the sort of imperfect, self-attached life that they could not truly sacrifice for God's sake; now, in the fullness of life, they can make that sacrifice. At each indrawn breath, the Name of God in the Heart flares like a coal. At each breath released, the whole fire of manifest existence is blown out like a candle.

# V

## LOVE AND KNOWLEDGE ON THE FIELD OF SPIRITUAL COMBAT

*A Comparison of the Sufi
Teachings of Javad Nurbakhsh
and Frithjof Schuon*

The day this heart placed its reins
In the hand of your love,
I gave up the desire for an easy life.
(The wise would lose their minds --
If wisdom only knew.)

The Gardens of Paradise draw life
    from the Garden of Union;
From the tortures of separation,
    one burning drop
Kindles all the fires of Hell.

[*after Hafiz*]

# LOVE AND KNOWLEDGE ON THE FIELD OF SPIRITUAL COMBAT

## A Comparison of the Sufi Teaching of Javad Nurbakhsh and Frithjof Schuon

### INTRODUCTION

THE OBSERVANCE of one's initiatory vows and a receptivity to the *baraka* one's lineage and spiritual Master make up the operative reality of the Sufi path. Yet an understanding of 'pure' metaphysics may also be of use on that path, as long as we realize that ideas alone, without practice, guidance and submission, can never alchemize the soul, even if the mental substance becomes receptive enough to catch a few lightning-like flashes from the spiritual Heart. To acquire a speculative knowledge of the eternal metaphysical principles can be a great support on the path—yet the operative essence of the path is not the fleeting intuition of changeless realities, but the progressive, methodical and *permanent* removal of the subjective, psychic obstacles to the manifestation of objective Love and Truth. When the will is submitted to God, the soul is pacified; when the soul is pacified, the Eye of the Heart opens.

In the words of the Qur'an (41:53), God says *We will show them Our signs on the horizons and in themselves, till it is clear to them that it is the truth. Suffice it not as to thy Lord, that he is witness over everything?* In other words, God absolutely transcends the division between inner and outer reality; His Love, His Knowledge and His Command appear equally in the realm the psyche and the realm of outer circumstances. Yet the 'horizons' do not only symbolize outer, material reality; they also represent the Truth of God as it dawns upon us from beyond the horizon of the subjective, psychic domain—in other words, the reality of metaphysical objectivity.

Being and knowing are ultimately One, which is why ontology (the science of being) and epistemology (the science of knowing), are inseparable. And psychology, especially in relation to the spiritual Path, is necessarily an aspect of epistemology. A spiritual state or station is always the reflection, or effect, of an objective metaphysical reality—a Name of God.

If we concentrate on ontology alone, without reference to our spiritual state—that is, without watching how the truths we witness are reflected in and affect our own souls—then our knowledge of God will remain purely mental or academic. But if, on the other hand, we attempt to witness and understand our psychic states without simultaneously recognizing them as reflections of objective realities, if we take them as entirely subjective—which postmodern philosophy and culture teach us to do—then we are ignoring Allah, and taking the *nafs* or unconscious ego as our god. The *nafs* can hide just as cunningly inside narcissistic self-intoxication, masquerading as asceticism or the love of God, as it can behind abstract mental knowledge, masquerading as gnosis. If the passional soul, the *nafs-al-ammara* is to be flushed from its hole, the army of metaphysical knowledge and the army of psychological self-understanding must meet, in a pincers movement, on a field whose center is the Heart, *al-Qalb*. The Arabic root QLB or QBL embraces a range of meanings that include turning around, turning toward, overturning and returning; according to the *hadith*,

> The hearts of the children of Adam are as if between the two fingers of the Infinitely Compassionate. He turns each however He wishes. O God, O Turner of hearts, turn our hearts toward obedience to You.

The Heart is part and parcel of the subjective psyche because it is always turning, this way and that. It is open, on one side, to the realm of contingency and becoming, but it is also the objective presence of God within the psyche, by which it may be seen that the Heart's turning is ultimately from God Himself. Self-understanding is the seed of objectivity, just as objectivity is the basis of self-understanding. If 'He who knows himself knows his Lord,' then he who knows his Lord also thereby knows himself.

Everything in the postmodern world works to tear apart epistemology and ontology, knowing and being—and only a sacred, *ontological psychology* can stitch them together again. Sacred psychology is the science of how the human soul is conformed, not only theoretically, but practically and existentially, to spiritual Truth. As such, it takes fully into account the conscious and unconscious barriers to such conformation, in the three realms of thought, feeling and will. It is, in other words, also an *operative epistemology*, in which Knowledge and Being are united—at which point, in the words of St. Thomas Aquinas, 'the Knower becomes the Thing Known'. And the fire which melts down the separation between Knowledge and Being, and recasts them in One Form, is Love. It is this sacred psychology that Dr. Javad Nurbakhsh, who always speaks in terms of the classical science of Sufism, presents in every one of his books.

## I. KNOWLEDGE OF GOD

The ways of knowing God are three: philosophy, theology, and *gnosis* or intellection; gnosis may be expressed—given that the gnostic is commanded to express it—in terms of metaphysics and/or theosophy. *Philosophy*—true philosophy—is speculation on the nature of being and the ways of knowing it, as well as the on cosmological laws and the ethical consequences that flow from such speculation—which is why philosophical knowledge must include self-knowledge; as the Delphic Oracle taught the philosophers of Greece, *know thyself*. *Theology*—at least as the word is used in western Christendom—is rational speculation on the truths that God has revealed to us in Scripture, which is from a Source far above rational knowledge. *Metaphysics* is the science of first principles or eternal truths, ultimately based on that direct perception of spiritual Truth that the scholastic philosophers call 'intellection' and some of the Church Fathers, 'gnosis'—a knowledge that is sometimes, but not always, inspired by revealed scripture. *Theosophy* is the articulated wisdom flowing from intellection or gnosis directly, from the immediate witnessing of Divine Reality. It often embraces

a metaphysical cosmology as well, having to do with the relationship between God and His own Self-manifestation as the celestial,
psychic and material universes, including the spiritual, psychic and
physical aspects of our Human Form. The Human Form is the center and epitome of God's Self-manifestation in this world, and also
the ladder that leads from the manifest universe back to its Divine
Source. Philosophy and theology give us knowledge *about* God;
only *gnosis* (in Arabic, *ma'rifa*) opens us to knowledge *of* God,
where God Himself is both the Knower and the Known. (NOTE: In
Eastern Orthodox Christianity, the word *theoria* denotes a way of
being and knowing that is much closer to *theosophy* or *gnosis*, as I
have defined them, than the 'theology' of the western church. In the
west, theology is essentially speculative; in the east, it is both speculative and operative.)

❖

According to Dr. Nurbakhsh, the stage below true Sufism but above
rational or theoretical or particular knowledge is gnosis, *ma'rifa*,
knowledge of God, while the flower and essence of Sufism is the
Love of God, which is not other than the perfection of knowledge.
Knowledge has to come before Love, since in order to love anything
you first have to know it. And Love is the final fruit of Knowledge of
God, since to know God is to love Him. Furthermore, as Mai-
monides said, 'Love is the highest form of Knowledge,' since Love
delights to dwell upon its Object; to live in intimacy with Someone
is to know Him well.

In *Sufism: Meaning, Knowledge and Unity*, in the chapter
'Ma'refat, Knowledge of God,' Dr. Nurbakhsh has this to say:

According to some Sufis, ma'refat is comprehension or knowledge of 'the thing itself', of essential knowledge. In this essay,
however, the word is used to mean true knowledge of God.

A drop of spray cannot engulf the sea nor can the part compre-
hend the whole; thus, without doubt, man cannot know God in
a way that befits Him. The best proof of this is God's own saying,
'They measure not God with His true measure' (*Koran* 6:92;

39:67); and, as the Prophet has said, 'we have not known Thee according to Thy true measure.'

Of course, with Divine help and grace, one may know God's attributes, at least to the extent of one's capacity. However, no-one can know god's Essence, his very Self, through his own limited selfhood. As 'Ali has said, 'I know God by God; I know 'other-than-God' by God's light.' (Nurbakhsh, 1981, p 44)

Imagine a ladder. The lowest rung is a theoretical knower who depends on the particular intellect, and the highest is a perfect Sufi. The knowers can be found between these two levels.

The more the knower depends on himself and his own knowledge, the lower the rung he occupies, but as he moves away from himself and his own knowledge, submitting more and more to God, he approaches the highest step. In reality then, the perfect knower and the perfect Sufi are one and the same. (Ibid., p 66)

In the words of Frithjof Schuon, 'Knowledge only saves us on condition that it enlists all that we are, only when it is a way and when it works and transforms and wounds our nature, even as the plough wounds the soil' (Schuon, 1954, pp 144–145).

Rational or particular knowledge is the Arabic *'aql* and the Latin *ratio*. *Ma'rifa*, on the other hand, is *gnosis*, based on the transcendent faculty known in Latin as *Intellectus* and in Greek as *Nous*, and called by both Sufis and Eastern Orthodox Christians 'The Eye of the Heart'. The knowledge of the Heart does not proceed logically or imaginatively from premise to conclusion. It is immediate, like sense perception, except that it perceives not temporal events but eternal realities. It knows these realities just as the eye knows light.

❖

We westerners have over-developed our rational, mental intelligence at the expense of every other way of knowing; but rationality which denies the higher forms of knowing upon which it is based ultimately breaks down. This is why, in postmodern times, we have become obsessively cerebral, without necessarily any longer being able to think. We are addicted to words and images; we need more of them every day, faster and faster, in order to suppress our awareness of the devastating effects of our addiction to words and images. This is why theosophy and metaphysics can imbalance the postmodern western soul, if they are taken on the purely mental level—which they will be, initially, especially if we approach them through books. Thus Dr. Nurbakhsh emphasizes the development of the spiritual virtues and the purification and awakening of the spiritual Heart, over and above the explicit study of metaphysics. If gnosis results from purification, it is known for what it is, a gift of God. If metaphysical principles are first understood on the mental level, and then allowed to sink toward the Heart in hopes that they will be realized, the result will be very uncertain: first, because the study of metaphysics can be intoxicating to those open to it; it can produce quasi-spiritual states which, since the principles in question are solidly understood on the mental level—the level of the particular intellect, of the kind of knowledge that can be acquired through memory—may be mistaken for sta-tions of spiritual *gnosis*, which they certainly are not; second, because the vast gulf between even a good mental understanding of meta-physics and the dark, habitual mindset of profane secular society is a standing temptation to intellectual pride; and third, because the Heart must be purified in any case for a mental understanding of metaphysical principles to give way to true *gnosis*.

Yet if the mental level is not fed with lore about God, it will nec-essarily feed itself on something else—on *everything* else. If our minds are secular, profane, and therefore dissipated, they will exist as a veil concealing the Knowledge and Love of God. And God only knows whether the cold intellectual pride of the person with a purely mental understanding of metaphysics, or the demonic dissi-pation of the person whose mind is fed on the jagged, vicious images of secular culture, is the greater barrier.

Sufis have always maintained that union with God cannot be attained through books; nonetheless Sufis, including Dr. Nur-bakhsh, have always written books. According to one story, a Sufi was in the habit of going out at night with a powerful lantern which he placed in the middle of the crossroad, where it attracted swarms of moths. He himself, however, went off to the side of the road, where he pursued his own studies by the light of a single candle. Though his light was faint, it was sufficient—and he was certainly not troubled by moths!

This story points to the possibility of occupying the mind with the lore of God so as to weaken its ability to distract the Heart from the contemplation of God. Lore-knowledge is not in itself the stable witnessing of Reality in any degree, and it can certainly become a serious distraction in itself. But under the right circumstances, God willing, it can support the witnessing of Reality by luring the mental substance away from its worldly dissipation, and concentrating it upon at least the reflected light of spiritual Truth.

And this is true to an even greater degree of the study the Qur'an. To listen to the recitation of it is even more powerfully recollecting than the study of metaphysics, since it is addressed to all levels of the human being, body, soul, Heart and Spirit. Awash in the abrupt and lightning-like periods of those Divine verses and signs, the wandering dog of the attention is brought swiftly to heel.

## II. STATES AND STATIONS
### FROM THE STANDPOINT OF KNOWLEDGE

Dr. Nurbakhsh teaches that Sufism is a school of humane conduct, concentration upon God and forgetfulness of self. He defines the spiritual Path (insofar as it can be systematically defined) in accordance with classical Sufi authorities, as made up of states and stations. Spiritual states are gifts of God; spiritual stations are acquired through our own efforts—with the proviso that all things, ultimately, are God's gifts, that even our own existence can in no way be attributed to us, any more than we can claim it as a personal achievement. Our existence is a free gift of His Existence to our essential nothingness. Spiritual states can be thought of as announcements of potential stations, while spiritual stations are, in one sense, states which have become crystallized, so that they form a permanent part of the human character.

The sacred psychology of spiritual states and stations makes up a great part of the science and lore of Sufism. But if we are essentially nothing, then who is experiencing those spiritual states and acquiring those spiritual stations? And if the practice of Sufism is based on forgetfulness of self, doesn't its expression in terms of the psychology of states and stations work against that forgetfulness? If I have acquired a particular station or am experiencing a particular state, and I know it—since unconscious states are not states at all, and unconscious stations, things that no-one could attempt to acquire through conscious effort—doesn't this build up my sense of separate selfhood rather than doing away with it?

This certainly would be true, except for the fact that states and stations are actually unveilings of the Names and Qualities of God, as well as intimations of God's hidden Essence, unknowable in Its fullness by anyone but God Himself. States are temporary unveilings of Reality, or unveilings which, though they may be long-lasting, have not yet alchemized the substance of our soul (i.e. our intellect, feelings and will), while stations are intimations become *certainties*: Whatever we really know about Reality compels us; we become the servants, the slaves of it because we are forced to take it into account. More than mere subjective experiences, then, states and stations are also objective realities. They affect and transform our psychic subjectivity because they come from beyond it, and above it. They dominate that subjectivity, just as an event of great joy or terror will snap us out of subjective daydreaming (in terms of states), or as, when driving a car, we have to take into account the objective layout of the city streets (in terms of stations). If they weren't objective aspects of the One Reality, states and stations would be nothing but the fantasies of the lower self, the *nafs*.

It is said that the realized Sufi is beyond states and stations. What does this mean? In subjective terms, it means that his ego-attachments and identifications, the knots and blockages in his psycho-physical system, have all been burnt out. Wherever there is such an ego-knot, a spiritual state or unveiling supervenes to undo it. When that knot is untied, the state is finished with and does not return again; that particular 'place' in the soul is now a station, a permanent trait of one's character. For example, neurotic fear (an ego-knot), burnt out by *states* of ecstatic love, becomes the *station* of courage and equanimity. But when a state keeps returning in such a way that a given ego-knot gets tighter instead of looser, as with any addiction, you can be sure that no matter how ecstatic or apparently enlightening the state appears to be, it is not really a spiritual state but a demonic fantasy of the *nafs*.

In objective terms, the realized Sufi is beyond states and stations because, in his case, the objective truth that God is the Only Being has been unveiled. When there is no-one there to be the subject of states and stations, how can they occur? Paradoxically, however, it is precisely the objective Truth of God, during the process of dawning upon us, that affects the soul with spiritual states and stations. What else could have the power? Illusion cannot enlighten itself. Reality (God) seems to dawn upon illusion (me), but it can't really do so without dispelling the illusion of my separate selfhood. Reality can only truly dawn upon Reality, and it has in fact already done so, from all eternity. Spiritual stations, therefore, are the qualities of God, not the qualities of man. It is said that the human soul is 'qualified by God's qualities'; yet it is only God who is ultimately the subject and ground of these qualities; the human soul is only the mirror of them. If this is not clearly enough understood, one may become a connoisseur and collector of spiritual states and virtues, which will ultimately turn out to be nothing but the fantasies and pretensions of the *nafs al-ammara*, the 'ego which commands to evil'.

### III. KNOWLEDGE AND LOVE

Dr. Nurbakhsh speaks of the relationship between love and knowledge in these terms: 'In discussing Intellect and Love from the point of view of Sufism, what is usually meant by intellect is reason or the particular intellect. But, in fact, the perfection of Divine Love manifests itself as the Universal Intellect; the perfection of Love is the same thing as the Universal Intellect.' (Nurbakhsh 1978, p. 27) The particular intellect seeks to acquire knowledge, but whatever knowledge comes to us by Love is given, not acquired.

Nothing is more certain than that it is impossible to become a friend of God through metaphysical 'knowledge' acquired from books and other forms of hearsay. It can sometimes, or for some people, even be an impediment on the Path. As Lao Tzu reminds us in his *Tao Te Ching*: 'In the pursuit of knowledge every day something is acquired; in the pursuit of Tao every day something is dropped' (Feng and English 1972, Chapter 44). Nonetheless, the fact that Shah Nimatullah, the founder of the Nimatullahi Order, wrote a commentary on the doctrines of Ibn al-'Arabi, is good evidence that under the right circumstances metaphysical lore can be highly useful, given that a spiritual Master writes only to instruct others. And the example of Ibn al-'Arabi himself, 'the Pole of Knowledge', illustrates the truth that profound metaphysical knowledge, like that found in his densely-packed *Fusus al-Hikam* (*The Bezels of Wisdom*) is in no way essentially opposed to Divine Love, as manifested in the beautiful metaphysical/erotic poems of his *Tarjuman al-Ashwaq* (*The Interpreter of Ardent Desires*)—though we need to remember that the capacity to express metaphysical ideas or compose beautiful poems on divine subjects has little to do with one's true spiritual station. And some of the greatest Sufis, known and unknown, never wrote a word.

The famous Ibn Sina (Avicenna) however, a central figure in both Muslim and Western Christian philosophy, may illustrate the opposite possibility, at least according to one perspective. After his death, the Sufi master Ala al-Dawla al-Simnani saw the Prophet in a dream, and asked him: 'What do you say on the subject of Ibn Sina?' The Prophet replied, 'He is a man whom God caused to lose his way in knowledge.' Likewise the Sufi Baha al-Din al-Amili also dreamt of the Prophet, and asked him about the post-mortem condition of Ibn Sina. The Prophet answered: 'Ibn Sina wanted to reach God without me, so I touched his chest and he fell into the fire.' (Nasr, 1978, p194)

So acquired knowledge is certainly a two-edged sword, even if touched by the light of the Universal Intellect. It is equally certain, however, that the following two statements can never be made in objective sincerity: 'I know God quite well; I simply don't love Him,' and 'I love Him with all my heart, but I don't really want to know Him.' Since, according to the Qur'an, all things return to Allah— this being true of philosophical discourse as well as of human souls—we must nonetheless remember that no statement about God that contains the word 'I' can be entirely sincere either, in the ultimate sense, because 'I' is precisely the veil of God—unless that 'I' be recognized as God Himself, as in Meister's Eckhart's teaching, 'my truest "I" is God.' And without 'myself', the argument between Love and Knowledge has no place to hang its hat, given that the separation between the two is nothing but an illusion of the ego. In Rumi's words, from the *Mathnawi*: 'Now,' said the Friend, 'since thou art I, come in: there is no room for two I's in this house.'

❖

When attempting to describe the Nimatullahi Sufi path as I have experienced it from my own limited perspective, I often call it 'apophatic *bhakti*', two words which can probably best be translated as 'love for the inconceivable'.

The usual reaction to the juxtaposition of these two words is surprise, followed by either delight or bewilderment. Most people who are interested in mysticism know that the *bhakti-marga* in Hinduism is the path of love, as opposed to the path of knowledge, *jñana-marga*, and the path of action, *karma-marga*. But the usual idea of *bhakti* is that it requires a formal object, an image of God as the Friend, the Beloved, the one with the beauty-mark, the dark entangling tresses, and the bewitching eyes. Hafiz:

> *If that Shirazi Turkish maid*
> *Would take my heart into her hand*
> *I'd give Bokhara for the mole on her cheek,*
> *Or Samarkand.*

The idea that the path of *bhakti* can take one beyond form, that the greatest Beauty is the beauty of the Invisible—*Layla*, or Black Night—is a novelty to many people. I remember an exchange I had with Dr. Ralph Austin at one of the Berkeley conferences of the Ibn al-'Arabi Society. I maintained that the greatest beauty is invisible; he, that beauty, as a mode of *maya*, has entirely to do with the world of manifestation. All I could tell him was that, by all *sane* criteria, he was right.

As I have already pointed out, to approach mysticism with the mind is dangerous. Mystical ideas can be so fascinating to those sensitive to them that they can sometimes produce glimpses of the

Truth which take a person beyond himself, beyond his real stage of development. In the words of Frithjof Schuon, 'A cult of the intelligence and mental passion takes man further from truth. Intelligence withdraws as soon as man puts his trust in it alone. Mental passion pursuing intellectual intuition is like the wind which blows out the light of a candle' (Schuon, 1954, p132). Nonetheless, metaphysical ideas can sometimes clarify our experience by furnishing the mind with concepts accurate enough to prevent less accurate concepts from distorting that experience and veiling it. There is nothing more unfortunate, and ultimately unnecessary, than for a state of spiritual unveiling to run up against a mass of mental scruples which maintain that such things can't really happen.

❖

The writers of the Traditionalist School—René Guénon, Ananda Coomaraswamy, Martin Lings, Titus Burckhardt, Marco Pallis, Leo Schaya, Rama Coomaraswamy, Wolfgang Smith, Seyyed Hossein Nasr, Whitall Perry, Joseph Epes Brown, James Cutsinger, William Stoddart, Frithjof Schuon, Huston Smith, *et. al.*—are often identified with the doctrine that knowledge is higher than love. And this characterization is partly justified. As Martin Lings puts it (whose voice and personality radiated love, whether he knew it or not), speaking of the spirituality proper to our time, which he terms 'the extreme old age of the macrocosm':

> the esoterism in question could not be other than what the Hindus call *jñana-marga,* the way of knowledge, or, more precisely, of gnosis. It was fated to be so, for such a way presupposes a perspective of truth rather than love, and it is objective regard for truth which characterizes the wisdom of old age. (Lings, 1987, p77)

I believe the Traditionalists exalt knowledge above love because they often limit love to a passionate and sentimental *bhakti,* clearly inferior to a sober, elevated and all-comprehensive *jñana.* Frithjof Schuon, however, maintained that 'Perfect love is "luminous" and perfect knowledge is "hot". . . . In God Love is Light and Light is Love'

(Schuon, 1954, p148), and taught that 'The way of love—methodical *bhakti*—presupposes that through it we can go toward God; whereas love as such—intrinsic *bhakti*—accompanies the way of knowledge, *jñana*, and is based essentially on our sensitivity to the divine Beauty' (Schuon 1991, p. 118). 'Where there is Truth, there is also Love', Schuon wrote. 'Each Deva possesses its Shakti; in the human microcosm, the feeling soul is joined to the discerning intellect, as in the Divine Order Mercy is joined to Omniscience; and as, in the final analysis, Infinitude is consubstantial with the Absolute.' (Schuon, 1986, p194)

Nonetheless, the doctrine that *jñana* is higher and more complete than *bhakti* surfaces again and again in the writings of Schuon and others of his school. And although this doctrine may generate an unwarranted bias against love in some people, I believe that there is a sense in which it is intrinsically true, though to understand exactly how it is true requires a 'revisioning' of what *bhakti* and *jñana* really are.

To begin with, they aren't absolutely bound to spiritual temperament, though this will always be an important factor. It is possible for *jñana* and *bhakti* to coexist within the same individual, depending upon whether he or she is in a state of or contemplative 'sobriety' or ecstatic 'drunkenness'. Furthermore, some contemplatives may pass through a station that could be called 'bhaktic' and arrive at one that is 'jñanic', as in the Sufi doctrine of 'sobriety after drunkenness'; *jñana* itself could be described, in the words of St. Augustine, as a kind of 'sober inebriation'. According to the Vedanta, devotion to God may open out, in the course of the spiritual Path, into a permanent contemplative realization in which God is the *atman*, the absolute Witness (cf. the Qur'an, 41:53). And we should remember that Shankaracharya himself, the greatest exemplar of *jñana* in Hinduism, wrote devotional songs.

C. F. Kelley, in *Meister Eckhart on Divine Knowledge*, distinguishes between a bhaktic, or affective, or 'relational' mysticism, such as that of Francois de Sales or St. John of the Cross, based on 'a gazing at, a looking at' its Divine Object (Kelley, 1977, p15), and the *jñanic* mysticism of Eckhart, who could say: 'My truest 'I' is God.' But 'relational' is not always equivalent to 'affective'. Those of *jñanic* temperament will tend to see the subject/object duality of relational mysticism as inseparable from *bhakti*, as when Sri Ramakrishna—in whom, however, the distinction between *bhakti* and *jñana* was almost certainly transcended—said, 'the devotee wants to eat sugar, not become sugar.' The knower is one with Knowledge, but the lover must remain in polarity with the Beloved for Love to exist. But *advaita* (non-dual) *bhaktas*—a definition which probably includes most Sufis—tend to have the opposite perspective: that it's really *jñana* which cannot exist without the subject/object polarity, because in the way of Knowledge the Knower must soberly contemplate the Known, while in the drunkenness of Love all separation between lover and Beloved is swept away in Union. However, as Dr. Nurbakhsh reminds us, perfect Love is identical to the Universal Intellect.

In the words of Sri Ramana Maharshi, the paramount *jñani* of modern times, '*Bhakti* is love for God with form; *jñana* is love for God without form.' This indicates that *jñana* cannot purely be limited to the perspective of knowledge as opposed to love, and would seem to imply the correlative, that *bhakti* cannot be reduced to a perspective of love as opposed to knowledge. What I have named 'apophatic *bhakti*' above, Ramana Maharshi apparently calls *jñana*. But if *bhakti* and *jñana* are not simply equivalent to love and knowledge, then what are they? To put it simply, *bhakti* is not strictly love as opposed to knowledge, but rather a *passion for God*, while *jñana* is not strictly knowledge as opposed to love, but rather serenity, sobriety and completion. It is important to note, however, that the bhaktic passion is 'passionate, not passional', a distinction William Blake epitomized when he wrote, in *Auguries of Innocence*:

> To be in a Passion you Good may do
> But no Good if a Passion is in you.

*Bhakti*, according to this definition, is the principle of relational mysticism, which is inseparable from a passionate desire both to know God *and* to unite with Him in love. Wherever there is duality there is passion, since the two must strive to become One, and by so striving continue to assert their twoness. But when the 'two' in question are the human soul and the Divine Reality, before which that soul is effectively nothing, the passion of this nothing to embrace that Reality in love, as well as encompass It in knowledge, is infinitely inflamed and infinitely frustrated at the same time, dissolving in ecstasy and returning to separation again and again, until it learns to temper its spiritual hunger, to submit to the will of the Beloved, to want whatever He wants even more than it desires union with Him on its own terms. This, incidentally, is the esoteric meaning of the 'beloved Lady hard-to-attain' in the traditions of the troubadours and the *Fedeli d'Amore,* where the Lady symbolized, and sometimes actually incarnated, the principle that all willful attempts at Union ultimately violate true love. God cannot be possessed or seduced, but must simply be obeyed, whether Her answer in a given spiritual moment be a sweet Yes, a bitter No, or a coy Not Yet.

*Jñana,* then, would be the principle of 'trans-relational' or *advaita* mysticism, in which God is both the Witness and That which is Witnessed. The *jñanic* gnosis is not cerebral as opposed to feeling-centered, but serene and complete as opposed to fragmentary and passionate, which is why Schuon, as we saw above, can distinguish between methodical *bhakti,* which expresses itself in relational mysticism, and intrinsic *bhakti*, which is inseparable from *jñana*. Furthermore, when Schuon writes

> What is 'love' at the start will appear as 'Knowledge' in the result, and what is 'knowledge' at the start will appear in the result as 'Love' (Schuon, 1954, p148),

the context permits the interpretation that he is speaking not only about two different individuals, a 'knower' and a 'lover', but also about the final spiritual destiny of thought and feeling within the same soul.

In *Survey of Metaphysics and Esoterism*, Schuon expresses the difference between a 'bhaktic' consciousness which contemplates the Divine Object and is finally absorbed into It, and a 'jñanic' one where the Divine Subject takes precedence, placing the second perspective higher than the first. He says:

> when the perception of the Object is so intense that the consciousness of subject vanishes, the Object becomes Subject, as is the case in the union of love; but then the word 'subject' no longer

has the meaning of a complement that is fragmentary by definition; it means on the contrary a totality which we conceive as subjective because it is conscious. When we place the emphasis on
objective Reality—which then takes precedence in the relation
between the subject and the object—the subject becomes object
in the sense that, being determined entirely by the object, it for-
gets the element consciousness; in this case the subject, inasmuch
as it is a fragment, is absorbed by the Object inasmuch as it is a
totality, as the accident is reintegrated into the Substance. But the
other manner of seeing things, which reduces everything to the
Subject, takes precedence over the point of view that grants pri-
macy to the Object: if we adore God, it is not for the simple reason
that He presents Himself to us as an objective reality of a dizzying
and crushing immensity—otherwise we would adore the stars
and nebulae—but it is above all because this reality, a priori
objective, is the greatest of subjects; because He is the absolute
Subject of our contingent subjectivity; because He is at once all-
powerful, omniscient and benefic Consciousness. (Schuon, 1986,
pp 39–40)

[in] the infinite and absolute Subject whose Object is on the one
hand its own Infinitude and on the other its Universal Unfold-
ing, there is no scission into subject and object on any ontological plane whatever ... for in this case the Subject is not a
complementary pole, it is simply That which is. If we nonetheless term it 'Subject', it is to express that *Atma* is the absolute Witness, at once transcendent and immanent, of all things. ...
(Ibid., 1986, p 39)

In describing this shift of emphasis from the human subject contemplating a Divine Object into which he or she is ultimately
absorbed, and the 'transformation' of this Object into the Absolute
Subject, the *atman,* Schuon is not simply presenting different spiritual perspectives; he is also, and necessarily, talking about successive
stages in the spiritual Path. And it is only in terms of this development from relational to *advaita* mysticism, starting from the sub-
ject/object duality, moving though absorption in the Absolute
Object, and culminating in the realization of the Absolute Subject

which, in contemplating the universe, gazes on nothing but Itself, that *jñana* is higher than *bhakti*. In terms of permanent spiritual stations, *jñana* comes after *bhakti*, but in terms of temporary spiritual states, they can alternate. Sometimes God is 'the other' in terms of my consciousness; at other times the human form—still, for sake of convenience, designated by my name—appears in the mirror of God's consciousness.

The practice of remembrance of God through invocation of His Name, central to Sufism (as *dhikr*) and Orthodox Christian Hesychasm (as *mnimi Theou*, usually in the form of the Jesus Prayer), and common as well in Hinduism (as *japa-yoga*), encompasses both *bhakti* and *jñana*. On the bhaktic level, I invoke God's Name, hoping He will unveil His presence. On the jñanic level, God speaks His own Name within me. The human form *is* God's Name in a sense; through the eyes of the human being who remembers Him, God names all things in manifest existence as aspects of Himself.

In the Vedanta, this development is presented in terms of four stages of realization: 1) *The universe is unreal, Brahman is the Real* [where the universe includes the human subject, which still 'exists', though it is recognized as an illusory—in Buddhist terms, devoid of self-nature; in Sufi terms, too 'poor' to claim self-existence]; 2) *There is only Brahman* [both the human subject and the universe it perceives are annihilated]; 3) *I am Brahman* [the 'place' of the human subject is now 'occupied' by the Witness, the *atman*]; and 4) *All this is Brahman* [the Witness witnesses all things as Itself]. And this development, far from being a motion away from love and toward knowledge, is actually a motion toward the union of love and knowledge, since in Brahman, the Divine Essence, love and knowledge are One. In the words of Ramana Maharshi, 'Imperfect *jñana* and imperfect *bhakti* are different; perfect *jñana* and perfect *bhakti* are the same.'

In one sense, it is impossible for 'me', who am nothing, to love God, Who is more than everything, any more than a gnat can make love to an elephant. There is no equality between the terms, no 'middle ground'—unless the spiritual Master, as a living representative of the Logos, is in fact that ground. As Dr. Nurbakhsh says in one of his poems, 'The Beloved is alive/ And the lover is dead.'

Nonetheless, on the Path of Love many images of the Beloved are generated, a new one in each *waqt*, each present moment of spiritual time; and as the *Shaykh al-Akbar* ('greatest of Sufi shaykhs') Ibn al-'Arabi teaches, God is willing to accept the worship paid to this momentary 'God created in belief' as if it were actually He. But it is not actually He, except in essence; and as the lover comes to realize this, his love expands into the Absolute Transcendence of God until all sense of the lover's psyche or personal identity is burned away; the moth (*psyche* in Greek) is consumed in the flame of the candle. This is the Sufi *fana*. But the candle, the Absolute Witness, still remains as Witness to the universe, which is none other than He— and what should He see in the foreground but the little human identity, still there, still composed of body, speech and mind, essentially unchanged, except for the fact that it is no longer 'me'. This is subsistence-in-God, the Sufi *baqa*. Ibn al-'Arabi says of this station, referring to 'divine gifts that . . . stem . . . from the Essence':

> they can result only from a Divine Self-revelation, which occurs only in a form conforming to the essential predisposition of the recipient of such a revelation. Thus, the recipient sees nothing other than his own form in the mirror of the Reality. He does not see the Reality Itself, which is not possible, although he knows that he may see only his [true] form in it. . . . If you have experienced this [in the spirit] you have experienced as much as is possible for created being, so do not seek to weary yourself in any attempts to proceed higher than this, for there is nothing higher, nor is there beyond the point you have reached aught except the pure, undetermined, unmanifested [Absolute]. In seeing your true self, He is your mirror and you are His mirror in which He sees His Names and their determinations, which are nothing other than Himself. (Austin, 1980, p 65)

Meister Eckhart says exactly the same thing: 'The eye through which I see God, and the eye through which He sees me, are the same eye.'

The entire story of the path leading from relational mysticism through annihilation in God to the unveiling of the Absolute Witness is told in the famous *hadith* of the Prophet Muhammad (peace and blessings be upon him): *Pray to God as if you saw Him*—relational mysticism—*because even if you don't see Him*—annihilation in God—*He sees you*—subsistence before the face of the Absolute Witness.

❖

Dr. Nurbakhsh, seemingly in opposition to the Traditionalists, places Love above Knowledge. The Sufi, as God's perfect lover—or rather, as the *locus* where the Beloved, the Lover and Love are recognized as none other than God Himself—is on a higher station than the gnostic or *arif* who has learned mystical secrets through direct unveiling, and stored them in his heart like precious jewels, just as the *arif* is on a higher station than the academic or religious scholar, limited to the particular intellect, who has gained all his or her knowledge through hearsay. As Nurbakhsh says in one of his poems, 'Where love is, there are no secrets.' But where all secrets are revealed, knowledge too must be perfect: 'In reality . . . the perfect knower and the perfect Sufi are one and the same.' (Nurbakhsh, 1981, p66)

So if both perfect knowledge and perfect love describe the perfect Sufi, is not the language of love enough, for those who have ears to hear it? Why speak of spiritual knowledge, with all its dangers of intellectual pride and mental greed, if Love is both *tariqa* and *haqiqa*, both the Path and the Goal? The reason is that gnosis is the only guarantee of objectivity; and without objectivity, love (or what passes for love) will inevitably be narcissistic and self-referential—under the power of the commanding *nafs*. Unless Divine Love is perfectly objectified—which does not mean 'transformed into a mere object' but rather 'freed from the limiting subjectivity of the one witnessing it'—then the lover, at least to a degree, will be in love with his or her own reactions to God, not with That One alone. One may temporarily lose oneself in intoxication, ravished by the beauty of the Beloved, only to return to the painful sobriety of (apparent) self-existence, over and over again. The only way out of this vicious cycle is the intoxicating sobriety of gnosis, in which Love is purified of the emotional reactions, the whining and pleading of the drunken lover, by being recognized as *al-Haqq*, the Truth. In the words of Frithjof Schuon, 'The love of the affective man is that he loves God. The love of the intellectual man is that God loves him; that is to say, he realizes intellectually—but not simply in a theoretical way—that God is Love.' (Schuon, 1954, p149) In the words of Hujwiri, from his *Kashf al-madjub*, 'Intoxication is to imagine that you have undergone annihilation, while in reality your own attributes remain. Thus, it is a veil. Sobriety, however, is a vision of your subsistence at the same time when your attributes have been annihilated. Thus, it is true unveiling. . . . The sobriety of heedlessness is the greatest of veils, while the sobriety of Love is the most manifest unveiling.' (Nurbakhsh, 1985, pp73–74)

The element of gnosis doesn't necessarily require a sophisticated philosophical mind—though the most sophisticated philosophies, or theosophies, that we possess are those produced by gnostics. All we need is the firm certainty that God is objectively real; the knowledge that we are absolutely dependent upon Him, instant-by-instant, for our very existence; the intuition that God sees and knows us, in this very moment, infinitely better than we can know either ourselves or Him; the perception that God's knowledge of us is in fact our essential reality; and finally the realization that what we call 'me' is fully objective to that Divine Witness within us, Who (in Eckhart's words) is 'our truest I,' given that 'he who knows himself knows his Lord.' Once this truth is realized, all philosophical and metaphysical speculation becomes unnecessary.

## IV. THE SUFI DOCTRINE OF THE *NAFS*

If Sufi doctrine is made up both of a metaphysics capable—up to a point—of alchemizing the psyche, and an operative psychology based on objective metaphysical principles, then the understanding of 'pure' metaphysics must always be complemented by an understanding of the psychic 'knots' or barriers which, in a given individual, in a given place and time, or in terms of the human form itself as conditioned by the inherent limits of the material and psychic worlds, prevent those metaphysical principles from being understood intellectually, loved an the level of the affections, and submitted to on the level of the will. An understanding of these psychic knots, both in general terms and also as they specifically appear, both habitually and momentarily, in the case of an individual soul—particularly one's own—is called 'gnosis of the *nafs*'. The word *nafs* means 'soul', most usually in the sense of the unconscious ego. The Sufi idea of the *nafs* is close to the Freudian concept of the *id*, except for the fact that Freud's *ego* is also an expression of the *nafs*, as are certain unconscious and obsessive aspects of his *superego*; blind and compulsive moralism is just as much a product of unconscious egotism as is blind and compulsive vice.

In the course of the spiritual Path, the *nafs* is purified and refined. Various Sufis have spoken of different stages of this purification, some referring to three stages, others to as many as seven. Dr. Nurbakhsh speaks of four stages. According to his teaching, the *nafs* first appears as 'the commanding *nafs*', the lower passional soul which rules us on the basis of our own whims, desires and self-will, until we submit instead to God's rule and become true *Muslims*. Next appears 'the accusing *nafs*', the troubled conscience, which recognizes the evil of the commanding *nafs*, struggles against it but is ultimately powerless to overcome it. This is followed by 'the inspired *nafs*', which begins to have intimations of higher realities and is able to know and follow what is good for it. And the final development is the '*nafs*-at-peace', the individual self in perfect submission to the Will of God. Some authorities identify the *nafs*-at-peace with the Heart; at any rate, it opens onto the Heart, which is only firmly established as Heart when the Spirit, *Ruh*, has finally conquered the *nafs* and subdued it—when the *pneumatic* humanity gains power over and subdues the *psychic* humanity.

The work of subduing and refining the *nafs* is also the work of developing the virtues. Every virtue is the expression of a metaphysical principle existentially actualized within the soul, and one of the simplest and most powerful images of this actualization is the system of the 'six stations of wisdom' in the teachings of Frithjof Schuon. In *Stations of Wisdom*, Schuon presents this doctrine in terms of the six discrete dimensions—the passive and active aspects of the will, the affections and the intelligence respectively, in their highest mode of operation. On the level of the will, purity and detachment are intrinsically paired with spiritual combat against the passions; on the level of the affections, peace and the contemplation of spiritual beauty are intrinsically paired with the fervent desire to be united to the Beautiful; on the level of the intellect, discrimination between the Real and the unreal is intrinsically paired with complete identification with the Real.

The Six Stations of Wisdom comprise an usurpassed and radiant image of the spiritual virtues as emanations of the Real addressed to our particular human faculties. Yet this image has a tendency to remain in a sort of ideal or aesthetic suspension, far above the vicissitudes of actual psychophysical life. That some have been capable, God willing and with the help of initiatory method and *baraka*, of realizing these virtues I have no doubt. Yet Schuon's understanding of the *nafs-al-ammara*, the actual psychic tendencies which would militate against their realization, leaves something to be desired. In terms of a general critique of the modern world, his analysis of the collective *nafs* is of the highest value; yet as he himself admitted, he was no psychiatrist. For example, his presentation of spiritual combat as the active aspect of the spiritual will, whose passive aspect is detachment, is theoretically profound; yet for actual advice on how to carry on such combat, Nurbakhsh's *The Psychology of Sufism* is of greater value, in my opinion, given that it is understood that such combat cannot be learned from books, and is rarely effective without competent spiritual guidance.

❖

Once upon a time the prophet Muhammad (peace and blessings upon him), after returning with his warriors from battle, said to them: 'Now we return from the lesser holy war to the greater holy war'. 'What is the greater holy war?' they asked. 'The war against the soul', he replied. When the Prophet defined the greater *jihad* in these terms, he laid one of the essential foundation stones of Sufism.

All spiritual traditions recognize that one cannot contemplate Absolute Truth without a progressive victory over the distracting desires of the ego, which include everything from lust and anger at the lower end of the spectrum to the simple assertion of one's independent existence at the other. The 'enemies' of the singer in the psalms of David are one representation of this egoic soul. In

Christianity it is called the 'old Adam', and is sometimes symbolized as the dragon slain by St. George. The Buddhists portray it as the mass of *klesas* or psychic impurities, and often use the image of a mad, drunken monkey to dramatize its effect on human consciousness. Sufism however, with its doctrine of the *nafs*, may well possess the most sophisticated psychology of the passional soul ever developed, according to which the *nafs* is seen not only as a beast to be conquered, but also as a deceiver to be outwitted, a resource to be tapped, and a servant to be enlisted—just as, in one Christian icon of St. George, the princess rescued by the knight from the dragon ultimately binds the now docile beast with a blood-red cord tied about her waist, and leads him home.

The *nafs*, from one perspective, is the entire 'natural' human psyche, which, like an iceberg, is composed of a relatively small visible portion—the conscious ego—and a much larger invisible mass—the 'unconscious'. But the concept of the *nafs* in Sufi psychology differs from that of the soul or psyche in most other psychological or religious doctrines in that the psyche only 'constellates' as the *nafs al-ammara,* the 'soul commanding or inciting to evil', after one has committed one's life to the spiritual Path. Before then the psyche will produce pleasant or unpleasant, constructive or destructive effects. It may be 'maladjusted' in social terms or relatively better-adjusted; it has certain virtues, certain vices, certain potentials, and various tendencies which are not well-formed enough to clearly belong to either camp. But when God has become the conscious center of one's life, then—as in a time of civil war—the various citizens of the psyche are forced to take sides. The commanding *nafs* only reveals itself as 'commanding' when we have begun to disobey it.

Since the *nafs* in its first stages represents all that comes between us and God, all that perverts our will so that we do not obey Him, or darkens our intellect so that we cannot intuit His Reality, a war without quarter against this *nafs* becomes imperative—the 'war against the soul'. But from another point of view, things are not quite so simple.

The position of humanity in the hierarchy of being is unique, a position which Islam defines by saying that we are both *abd,* God's abject slave, and *khalifa,* God's fully-empowered representative. In a certain sense, we bear the responsibility for the maintenance of the cosmic order. As it says in the Qur'an, *We offered the Trust to the heavens and the earth and the hills, but they shrank from bearing it and were afraid of it. And man assumed it* (33:72). The Trust is our essential duty to act as mirrors for God in the created universe—and while we are in the grip of the *nafs*, which causes us to believe that we are self-created, and therefore that we have the right to be self-determined, we cannot fulfill this function. But we can't literally destroy this *nafs*, nor can we conquer it. We can't conquer it because the 'we' in question is itself part of the *nafs*, the part that is entirely capable of perverting spiritual struggle so as to build up an apparently separate identity instead of annihilating it. Nor can we destroy it, because the *nafs* is created by God Who wills its existence, and a war against the will of God is lost before it begins.

So is God then a tyrant and deceiver, who has put us in a hopeless double-bind by commanding us, on pain of hellfire, to kill the ego—something which He knows to be impossible because He Himself opposes it? Certainly, the tyrannical and deceiving *nafs* will tend to falsely represent Him in these terms. Nonetheless, it is true that God has commanded us, in one sense, to struggle against the current of His Self-manifestation in order to reach Him, just as a salmon must swim upstream against the current of the river to reach its Source.

The *nafs* is the trace in our nature of God's original creation of the universe, of his command *kun*, 'be!', addressed to all the things that have come into being. If we follow this current, which is the 'natural man' or 'old Adam' within us, we will live only to express ourselves, to develop and enhance our existence, and end by burning ourselves out in dissipation and flight from God, like sunlight that becomes ever dimmer in its flight from the Sun. What could be more 'natural'? This is, in fact, what the whole cosmos is doing, according to the theory of an expanding universe originating in a 'big bang'. It is simply following the law of entropy, dissipating itself, burning itself out in order to manifest on the material plane certain possibilities latent within the Divine Nature, and thereby fulfilling its function, as expressed in the famous *hadith qudsi* in which God says: 'I was a hidden Treasure and longed to be known, so I created the universe that I might be known'. But in a negative but no less lawful sense, the expanding, entropic universe is precisely 'the heavens and the earth and the hills' in flight from the Trust. The universe is God's manifestation; the power which manifests the Divine Nature—in Hindu terms, *Vidya-Maya*—also necessarily veils It by appearing to be something other than Him—*Avidya-Maya*.

The universe outside humanity, though it does indeed mirror God, mirrors Him in a fragmentary way, as does a human psyche when in the grip of the *nafs*. The material universe, composed of whirlpools of galaxies and throngs of living species and swarms of elementary particles, of energies and their fields, and the human consciousness made turbulent by passions and attachments, are like a lake on a windy day. The light of the Sun reflected in such a lake appears as a million dancing sparks of light. But when the wind sinks, and the lake becomes calm, then the Sun is reflected as a single unified form. This ability of the human spiritual Heart to reflect God in His entirety—and on the basis of this perfect mirroring to contemplate the material universe as ultimately composed of nothing but the 'signs' of Allah—is the Trust which That One has laid upon us. It is the reason why He created us in the first place, and why He has sent prophets and avatars to instruct us and religious revelations to enlighten and save us. The soul which has become calm like a lake on a bright and windless day is the '*nafs*-at-peace', which is also sometimes identified with the spiritual Heart. The Heart in Sufism is not quite the fullness of the *atman* or Divine Self of Vedantic Hinduism (which is perhaps better translated by the Sufi terms *sirr*, 'secret', just as *sirr al-sirr*, 'the Secret of the secret', may refer to the Absolute Essence as It is in Itself, beyond even the divine act of witnessing, the reality that the Hindus call *Brahman*), but is more like what Jung was groping toward in his concept of the 'Self archetype'—the 'central' point of the psyche where it is intersected by a ray of the Spirit radiating from Allah, the Absolute Witness, the Divine Self. (In the Qur'an 41:53, which we have already quoted above, Allah is identified as the Absolute Witness: 'We will show them Our signs on the horizons and in themselves, till it is clear to them that it is the truth. Suffice it not as to thy Lord, that He is witness over everything?') The Heart is thus the border between the realm of psychic multiplicity and that of Spiritual Unity. As it is said in the *hadith qudsi,* 'Heaven and earth cannot contain Me, but the heart of my believing slave can contain Me.'

In another sense, however, even the *nafs*-at-peace remains under Divine Wrath, since it still manifests a trace of separate existence. The ego, no matter how submissive, cannot attain Union with God. When a young man told the Sufi woman saint Rabi'a that he had never committed a sin, her answer was: 'Alas, my son, thine existence is a sin wherewith no other sin may be compared.'

God has two mercies: *Rahman* (equivalent in some ways to *Avidya-Maya*), His general mercy, by which He creates the universe, and *Rahim* (closely equivalent to *Vidya-Maya*), His particular mercy, by which He leads all things back to Himself. *Rahman* is general because it says 'yes' to everything; *Rahim* is particular because it says 'yes' to beliefs and actions which bring us closer to God and 'no' to beliefs and actions which drive us further away. By *Rahman*, God grants the wish of all possible things to be actualized; He bestows upon them the life and reality they long for. The joy of sexuality and the fear of death are the measure of the depth of this longing. But the desire for separate existence, which begins as a mercy, ends under the sign of wrath: departing from God, or rather from the knowledge that God is the only Reality, created beings end up in the outer darkness, subject to evils and sufferings of all kinds, and they cry to God for relief. In response to this cry, God unveils *Rahim*, which manifests in terms of religions, and sacred laws, and prophets, and saints, and the spiritual Path. All creation cries to be saved, and *Rahim* mercifully dawns to show the Way back to God, the sovereign Good, the only Reality. The mercy of creation is general because it encompasses all things. The mercy of divine revelations such as the Qur'an is also general to a degree because it is addressed to an entire community—yet within it are the seeds of a particular mercy, one addressed to 'myself' alone and only fully manifest as *tariqah,* the spiritual Path. And even though the work of this Path is the conquest of the *nafs,* the annihilation of 'myself', nonetheless, without the appearance of 'myself', the spiritual crisis which heralds the dawn of God's particular mercy, and ultimate the return of all creation to Him, could not take place. Though revelations are given to whole religious communities, no community as a whole ever became a saint.

*Religion* is God's wish that we abandon attachment to His general and creating mercy, and commit ourselves to His particular and saving mercy. Only humanity is confronted with this choice. The animals, the plants, the minerals are fixed under *Rahman*. The angels made their choice in pre-eternity, and those who have retained angelic status remain rapt in the contemplation of God. Only humanity can consciously choose, by God's grace, to shift our center-of-gravity from *Rahman* to *Rahim*, this choice being the essence of the spiritual Path. We are required, in other words, to break identification with one of God's mercies and avail ourselves of the other, which means that, according to the doctrine of Ibn al-'Arabi, we must stop living on the basis God's *will* to send us out into creation, manifest as our God-given instincts—a will that is essentially nothing but God's perfect fulfillment of our own desire—and grant His *wish* that we abandon our own desire and return to Him—a wish which is nothing but His compassionate response to our own cry for help. In terms of the spiritual psychology of the Sufi way, we must purify the Heart so that the army of the Spirit may take possession of it from the army of the *nafs*. All this is epitomized in the passage from the Qur'an, 'There is no refuge from God but in Him' (9:118).

The *nafs*, then, being the product of God's *Rahman*, is not evil in essence, though it is certainly the *source* of evil, which is why it is said in the Qur'an, *I seek refuge in the Lord of Daybreak from the evil of that which He created* (113:1–2). And in a larger sense, we can say that if God had not by His general mercy created the universe, His particular mercy would have no field of operation, just as a salmon, though it must fight against the current to swim upstream, would have no river to travel in if the water were not flowing downstream. And just as that fish, even though he is fighting against the current of the river, is also using it, so the goal of the alchemy of the Sufi path is to transmute the *nafs* from a mortal enemy into an obedient servant—not, of course, a servant of oneself (that is, of *itself*), but rather of one's Lord. This is why it Sufis say that first you have to repent—thus transforming the commanding *nafs* into the 'accusing *nafs*' or remorseful conscience, the field of the greater *jihad*—after which you will eventually have to repent of that repentance: the goal of war is not war without end, but victorious peace. This is the point at which the accusing *nafs*, the sign of the struggling ascetic, is transformed into the *nafs*-at-peace, the sign of the lover of God.

The war against the soul, against the commanding *nafs*, is a total war, and the enemy, even though in essence he is a product of God's mercy, is effectively merciless, profoundly destructive and infinitely more powerful than the puny 'spiritual' ego that wants to be wise or good or even self-annihilated by its own efforts and on its own terms, without God's help and the grace of one's spiritual Master. To fight the commanding *nafs* on the basis of one's self-will is doomed to failure, if for no other reason than that the self-will of the spiritual ego is itself an aspect of the commanding *nafs*—the aspect personified by the Sufis as Eblis, the Muslim Satan. Nonetheless, this impossible battle still has to be fought. The *nafs* must try to annihilate itself, try to attain God, simply because the spiritual traveler has to begin somewhere, and at the beginning of the spiritual Path the traveler is all *nafs*. This hopeless attempt at self-transcendence has the effect of transforming the primitive passions of the commanding *nafs*, based on the struggle for security, pleasure and power, into self-criticism and spiritual aspiration: the accusing *nafs*. The very energy of the lower passions is tapped for the purpose of traveling the spiritual Path. This transformation does not take place by self-will, however, but by the grace of God—yet insofar as we still believe we are self-determined, we must make full use of this fundamentally illusory self-determination, or no progress will be made. Dr. Nurbakhsh explains it in these terms, according to the paradox of free will and predestination: At the beginning of the Path, if the aspirant claims that everything happens by God's will he is an unbeliever; he must exercise his own free will and assume full personal responsibility for carrying out his spiritual duties. But if at the end of the Path he still claims to possess free will, he is again an unbeliever, since the goal of the Path is to witness how everything that happens is by God's will, since none other than God exists. (cf. Nurbakhsh 1996, p 80)

According to the *hadith qudsi*, God's mercy takes precedence over His wrath—which, in terms of the individual, means that submission is higher than struggle; the accusing *nafs* is superseded by the *nafs*-at-peace. Thus the goal, and one might say the 'environment' of the greater *jihad* is peace, submission, surrender—and absolute submission can only be made to the Absolute itself; this is indicated by the fact that the Arabic words *Islam*, 'submission', and *salaam*, 'peace, surrender', are from the same root. The ultimate end of submission is not simply submission of the will or the affections to God, but submission of one's very sense of separate existence. In Sufi terms, this is *fana*, annihilation-in-God, whose seemingly-opposite but actually complementary aspect is *baqa*, subsistence-in-God. To subsist in God is to know oneself as absolutely contingent upon the Absolute. It is to come to the end of self-determination and self-definition. In *fana*, the ego is killed; in *baqa*, it is realized that the ego need not be killed since it has never existed in the first place.

The saying of Jesus, 'he who seeks to keep his life shall lose it, but he who loses his life, for My sake, shall find it,' refers to precisely the same reality. When in the Qur'an Allah says, O *men! Ye are the poor in relation to God, and God is the Rich to whom all praises are due*, He is attributing all Being to Himself, and none at all to us—except *His* Being. The ego, then, is fundamentally a mis-perception; in Vedantic terms, it is nothing but an identification of the Absolute Witness with the body, or the will, or the feelings, or the mind. When the Absolute Witness is unveiled, this identification is broken—it was never there: a realization which Ramana Maharshi taught his students to demonstrate to themselves by attempting to witness the essence of ego, and thereby discovering that there is no ego to be witnessed. This is the essence of the Sufi doctrine that, in reality, only God exists. In the words of the Qur'an, *all is perishing except His face*.

## V. THE REMEMBRANCE OF GOD
### ON THE FIELD OF SPIRITUAL COMBAT

The Invocation of the Name of God, the *dhikr* of the Sufis (closely related to the Platonic *anamnesis*), is essentially the practice of remembering God and forgetting oneself. But it should always be emphasized that the Invocation of God's Name—in Sufi terms—can't be effectively practiced on one's own initiative; it can only be conferred through a valid initiation. In the words of Dr. Nurbakhsh,

'One can recite the words of zekr heard from anyone, but zekr itself can be bestowed only by a perfect master.' (Nurbakhsh, 1979, p34)

In regard to this, Ramana Maharshi tells the following story: A king once asked a sage why he couldn't simply practice a form of the Invocation he had discovered in a book. The sage responded by turning to a nearby courtier and shouting, 'Seize the king and bring him to me!' Not surprisingly, the courtier did not move. 'Seize him!' repeated the sage. The courtier remained frozen. Enraged, the king roared to the courtier, 'On the contrary, seize this so-called wise man and bring him to me!' The courtier obeyed instantly. 'Explain yourself or lose your head!' roared the king. 'Certainly, Your Majesty,' the sage replied. 'I was merely illustrating a point. The Invocation is effective only if it has authority behind it; if the would-be practitioner attempts to command it on his own non-existent authority, it will remain inert. Only the King can allow, and command, his subjects to approach him; *they* have no authority to demand that *he* approach them. The Invocation is the servant of God, not man—and of the spiritual Master who is God's representative.'

❖

The *hadith qudsi* quoted above—'Pray to God as if you saw Him, because even if you don't see Him, He sees you'—can also be taken to refer to three distinct levels of the *dhikr*.

To begin with, 'I' am speaking God's Name, struggling to remain conscious of Him, or asking Him to reveal His Presence—to 'me'. The 'God' I am dealing with on this level is what Ibn al-'Arabi called 'the God created in belief'. He is inseparable from my ego; in a way He is a projection of it; contemplating Him on this level is the same thing as contemplating myself: this is the meaning of '*as if* you saw Him'. Nonetheless, as Ibn al-'Arabi points out, God still accepts the prayers we make to our image of Him, even if that image is an illusion—because, in another sense, it really *is* Him. God, as the Essence of all forms, is indeed worshipped—though in a veiled way—through the worship paid to idols, even if the idol is our own ego. According to Shankaracharya, the ego, even though it is the veil over the Self, is also a sign of the Self. It is true that those who worship God in the form of their own egos experience Him as Wrath; but if they were to allow that Wrath to take them beyond the level of personal and religious idolatry, it would be revealed as a face of Mercy.

At a later stage of the *dhikr,* the one represented by 'even if you don't see Him,' we realize that our image of God is really only the projected shadow of our ego, and begin to encounter God as He is. At this point the words of Abu Bakr apply: 'To know that God cannot be known is to know God.' The limited, egotistical 'knower' is bewildered, neutralized; the unknowability of God consumes all our attempts to know Him in the fire of Knowledge itself; this is *fana*, annihilation in God. Here we are no longer invoking God's Name, but God is invoking His own Name within us. The Name no longer refers to a separate Object as perceived by a separate subject; God and His Name are One.

To catch a glimpse of the reality of God by forgetting yourself— or to remember God so completely that the individual self is forgotten for a moment—is to realize that you are seen more fully and more penetratingly by Him than you could ever see yourself. *Remember Me, and I will remember you* (Qur'an 2:152). And such Remembering in reality begins not with you, but with Him: *It is We who have sent down the Remembrance.* (Qur'an 15:9) To remember God until God is known as the only Rememberer is to become the mirror of Allah, and realize the Supreme Identity.

This is the final stage of remembrance, the stage of 'He sees you'. The limited subjective selfhood is first forgotten *(fana)* and then transformed into the object of God's remembering, an object which is fundamentally none other than God, since That One witnesses only Himself. This is the stage of 'subsistence in God' *(baqa),* which implies one's subsistence as a Name of God, with no independent self-existence other than His. And though it is the third and final stage of remembering, it is also virtual, and effective, from the beginning, because it is the Truth.

❖

According to Dr. Nurbakhsh, 'Sufis must confirm, seek and see only the Absolute Being and not think about anything else' (Nurbakhsh, 1996, p 27). But he also says, 'To attain God one must wage spiritual combat *(jehad)* with the *nafs*, and Sufis devote most of their time to this combat. . . .' At this point one might ask, if the essence of the path is to remember God and forget the ego-self, how can the Sufi spend most of his time in spiritual combat against the ego-self, the *nafs*? If you have declared war on someone, you had better pay very close attention to what he's up to.

One answer is that the decision to seek only the Absolute will necessarily bring up everything in one's soul which knows that it must die if the Absolute is ever actually found. Thus the practice of attention is largely the practice of becoming aware of distractions. In his chapter on *mohasebeh* (self-examination) from *In the Paradise of the Sufis*, and in *The Psychology of Sufism*, in the chapter on the *nafs*, Dr. Nurbakhsh makes it clear that attention to the states of one's ego is the necessary complement to concentration upon Absolute Being. Since the ego does not really exist, to be aware of it is to detach from it, to deny it the food it lives on, which is identification, whereas to be unconscious of it is to identify with it, and consequently to remain lost in the illusion of selfhood.

So at the very least we can say that the purpose of *dhikr* is not to build a fantasy-palace of spiritual comfort with walls so thick that the clamoring of the *nafs* is drowned out, leaving the soul in a state of complacency and self-satisfaction which is mistaken for spiritual peace; such an attempt is itself a deception of the *nafs*. The true practice is to be simultaneously aware of the Divine Name, which (in virtual terms) is God's real Presence within the soul, and of the reactions of the *nafs* to one's awareness of that Presence. In this simultaneous awareness, however, there is no essential division; to divide one's attention, giving part of it to God and another part to the *nafs*, would be to set up the *nafs* as a partner with God, this being the sin of *shirk*. In God's Presence, the attention is not divided but unified, since He is the One, the Real. God's presence is ultimately the Witness, and the Witness encompasses all that is witnessed, with no essential division between them. In that Presence, if we fully embrace it through self-forgetfulness (in the positive sense of sacrifice of one's self-concept, not the negative one of psychological repression, which is nothing but the self-imposed division of attention between what is acceptable to the ego and what is not), then the egoic patterns and deep feelings which arise are not something ultimately other than God, something that we always have to keep a separate lookout for, but are progressively revealed as realities which move like waves through the depths of the Divine Nature. They constitute what Frithjof Schuon calls *maya-in-divinis,* the pre-figuration of contingent being within, and as, Absolute Being. And Dr. Nurbakhsh was undoubtedly referring these realities, in terms of the Divine wrath experienced by the *nafs* in the process of being transformed into the action of God—and simultaneously being revealed as always having been that action—when he said that in the sea of Unity we should expect to encounter sharks from time to the time, since the perfection of the Ocean requires the existence of such creatures.

The purpose of *dhikr,* then, is not to let us rise above the *nafs* through identification with metaphysical Truth conceived of as a spiritual ideal, but rather to transmute the *nafs* on its own ground, so that it no longer veils that Truth. Spiritual idealism wants to rise, let us say, from the earth of materialistic 'ordinary life', first through the water of spiritual devotion and then through the air of metaphysical understanding, till it reaches the fire of identification with the Absolute; this is the very path taken by the *nafs* when it tries to 'spiritualize' itself. Dr. Nurbakhsh, however, presents the purification and transmutation of the *nafs* as a motion in the opposite direction:

> The wayfarer's progress at the spiritual level of the *nafs* is downward. This is to say at first, the commanding *nafs* is governed by a fiery nature. When it descends from this fieriness to become the blaming *nafs,* it becomes governed by airiness. Once it has descended from airiness and become the inspired *nafs,* it becomes governed by wateriness. Once it has descended from this watery nature and become the *nafs*-at-rest, it becomes governed by earthiness, gaining stability, whereupon it becomes characterized by humility, dignity, meekness and submissiveness. (Nurbakhsh, 1992, p67)

Remembrance of God transmutes the soul: will, feelings and thought. Because it is a constant and never-ending practice performed under vow of obedience, it pacifies and strengthens the will, thus accomplishing the first two of Schuon's stations of wisdom: detachment from all that is other than God, and combat against all that would distract one from the presence of God.

Because it is a Name which refers to and makes present a real Object, the invocation of the Divine Name transmutes thought. As Dr. Nurbakhsh puts it,

> The Sufi is attentive to the Name itself, as well as to its meaning or significance. This is necessary since human beings have the habit of being attentive to a concept by means of words. Thus, when a word is remembered, the corresponding concept tends to rise in one's awareness. Attention to the Name alone . . . is a kind of idol-worship' (Nurbakhsh 1979, p 20).

In the course of *dhikr*, by which we remember that God *Is*, ordinary dissipated thought is transmuted into the question, '*if* God is, then Who and What is God?' The asking and answering of this question continues, constantly changing, in the light of God's presence, until 'I-and-You' is transcended. In Sufism this spontaneous asking-and-answering, on a level deeper than discursive thought, where question and answer are not successive but simultaneous, is termed *fikr*, contemplation. In the words of Ruzbehan Baqli, 'Thought for the ordinary man is plunging in the sea of illusion, while contemplation for the elect is being immersed in the ocean of understanding.' (Ibid., p 56)

On the level of feeling, remembrance of God brings to consciousness the psychological knots or habitual patterns of psychophysical tension of which the *nafs* is composed. We have created these psychological knots to prevent ourselves from feeling our true feelings. These patterns of tension operate on the level of the emotions by making us either dissipated and manic, or congealed and depressed, or both. On the level of the will, they make us lazy and/or driven; on the level of thought they render our minds formless and chaotic, and also filled with hard fixed ideas—all for the purpose of hiding from us what we really feel, and what we might really know. They are very good at what they do.

One of the primary ways that *dhikr* cuts through this mass of *ghaflah*, this 'heedlessness', is by alchemizing the emotions. The practice is to use whatever emotions the *dhikr* brings up—fear, anger, sorrow, elation, mellowness, shame, disgust—any and every emotion which arises in a given moment, to deepen and empower the *dhikr*. Thus 'the obstacles become the Path'. In *dhikr*, the will is dedicated to constancy of practice and the intellect to attention. Once this dedication is established, the emotions rise and offer themselves to be transmuted. Initially they appear as distractions; ultimately they become food and fuel.

Emotions are energy; remembrance is attention. In tantric terms, emotion (on the level of pure contemplation) corresponds to an aspect of *Shakti,* and attention to a manifestation of *Shiva*. Attention invokes energy; energy empowers attention; the Union of attention and its energy is Liberation. Dr. Nurbakhsh describes this Liberation as follows:

> The *baqa* corresponding to inner *fana* [annihilation in God's Essence, as opposed to outer *fana*, annihilation in His Acts] is one in which the very veils that are the temporary essence and attributes of the disciple's self are removed. Here, God neither veils the creation, nor does the creation veil God. The veil has been totally removed, and duality transformed into Unity. (Nurbakhsh, 1979, p 24)

The emotional and psycho-physical knots are the fuel; the remembrance is the fire.

The practice is to feed the fire. Feed those knots to the *dhikr* and it will burn brighter and hotter, bringing more and more psycho-physical knots smoking and bubbling to the surface.

Behind these knots of the *nafs* are true feelings, which are not to be confused with those so-called 'positive' emotions, or habits of auto-stimulation, that one is habitually using to distract oneself from emotional pain. These surface emotions are still part of the *nafs*; they are nothing but our way of avoiding the encounter with our psycho-physical knots, and are also a direct expression of these knots. Behind these knots of habitual self-avoidance are the true feelings themselves, the ones we may have spent a lifetime trying to stay unconscious of by distracting ourselves, creating false identities (which involve us with false situations in order to maintain and validate themselves) and generally polishing up our character-armor—notably *fear, hurt, anger* and *sadness*. No matter: feed them all to the *dhikr*. Posit them not as shameful vices or terrible illnesses or impenetrable barriers to God, but as elements of fervor, of longing for union with the Beloved. [NOTE: Depression, mania and panic are not feelings, but psycho-physical strategies for avoiding feelings. In depression we hide from them in a kind of auto-sedation; in mania we fly over the top of them; in panic we fight and/or flee them.]

On the level of the *nafs, fear* is the denial that all things must return to Allah because they are without self-identity, and He the only Reality. On the level of the Heart, it is vigilance in allowing no sense of self-existence to intrude upon the Presence of God. The fear of the *nafs* is transmuted into the vigilance of the Heart by means of Awe before God.

On the level of the *nafs, hurt* is the disappointment of expectations, the feeling of being teased, seduced or rejected by the person or situation we hoped to be united with. On the level of the Heart it is devotion to God as Beloved, whatever His actions may be, in the realization that, though He can never belong to us no matter what we do, we already belong to Him; it is to place ourselves in God's hands, 'like a corpse in the hands of a washer of the dead.' The hurt feelings of the *nafs* are transmuted into the Heart's submission to God's actions by the practice of accepting, in humility, all events *as* God's actions, and thus ultimately recognizing all events as veils and manifestations of Mercy: If God's Mercy has precedence over His wrath, then His wrath is necessarily a servant of His Mercy. Because God is the Sovereign Good, every way He moves us, every way he turns our Heart, is good for us; the experience of Divine Wrath is based on our resistance, not His intent.

*Anger* on the level of the *nafs* is the false arrogation to oneself of absolute power over circumstances, which is continually being frustrated, since we are not God; on the level of the Heart, it is God's righteous anger against this very arrogance, His overpowering demonstration that omnipotence is His alone. On page 47 of *The Psychology of Sufism*, Dr. Nurbakhsh identifies Satan with the human ego, the *nafs*. Satan is the one who cannot be and yet desires the prerogatives of being, which is why he must make his living as a thief. Thus the word *kun,* ('be!') is not only the word of creation, but also the word of exorcism. The anger of the *nafs* is transmuted into the Heart's righteousness through swift obedience to God's command.

*Sadness* on the level of the *nafs* is the feeling that one is lost in an empty world, and that there is nothing beyond this world; on the level of the Heart it is the ability to repose deeply in Being. The sadness of the *nafs* is transmuted into the Heart's repose by means of nostalgia for Eternity, longing for a distant Paradise, which culminates in the witnessing of the infinite generosity and abundance of God as present in this moment.

These four primal emotions are alchemized by God's grace consciously received and cooperated with, a transmutation that occurs on the border between God's real action and the apparent action of the *nafs*—in this case most likely the *nafs-e molhama,* the 'inspired nafs', which lies between the accusing *nafs* and the *nafs-*at-peace on the scale of spiritual development (see Nurbakhsh, 1992, pp 56–58).

This bare *schema* of the emotions and their transmutation certainly does not exhaust the subject. Every realized Sufi—and I am not among their number—will speak of the matter, if he or she is commanded to do so, in a different and unique way. My view is based on my own spiritual states, not yet free of subjectivity, plus the teachings of those wiser than I, and my own speculation on both that teaching and those states.

❖

It is important to understand that fear, hurt, anger and sadness are not only subjective reactions but also objective realities; they represent forces operating on the psychic plane, beyond their momentary appearance in this or that individual—forces that are themselves reflections of metaphysical principles located on the spiritual plane. The ultimate metaphysical roots of fear, hurt, anger and sadness are to be found on the level of the fundamental Divine Attributes; those who have a clear vision of these *hypostases,* as well as a vision of the nature of the *nafs* in light of them, will be able to deal with these primal emotions from a standpoint of transcendental objectivity.

From one perspective, the most fundamental divine *hypostases* are the Absolute and the Infinite. According to Frithjof Schuon,

> In metaphysics, it is necessary to start from the idea that the Supreme Reality is absolute, and that being absolute it is infinite. That is absolute which allows of no augmentation or diminution, or of no repetition or division; it is therefore that which is at once solely itself and totally itself. And that is infinite which is not determined by any limiting factor and therefore does not end at any boundary. . . .

> The Infinite is so to speak the intrinsic dimension of plenitude proper to the Absolute; to say Absolute is to say Infinite, the one being inconceivable without the other. . . .

> The distinction between the Absolute and the Infinite expresses the two fundamental aspects of the Real, that of essentiality and that of potentiality; this is the highest principial prefiguration of the masculine and feminine poles [Schuon, 1986, pp15–16].

According to Schuon, the Absolute is related to God's Transcendence, since it excludes, as non-existent, all that is other than Itself, and the Infinite to His Immanence, since there is no place where It is not. Yet it is equally possible to conceive of the Absolute vis-a-vis the relative, manifest world, as that Reality by virtue of which the very relativity of that world becomes apparent, and of the Infinite in and of itself, as a transcendent property of God alone, independent of formal manifestation—given that relativity, while virtually endless on its own plane, is composed of nothing but boundaries: only God is Infinite. Therefore we can say that the ultimate root of *fear* is the *transcendent Absolute*; of *hurt*, the *immanent Infinite*; of *anger*, the *immanent Absolute*; and of *sadness*, the *transcendent Infinite*. Before the transcendent Absolute, manifest existence has no 'rights'; it is as nothing; it is already annihilated. In the presence of the immanent Infinite, all expectations are frustrated; closure cannot be made; to either possess or reject the loved object is impossible, since She is simultaneously beyond one's grasp and at the root of one's desire. Before the immanent Absolute, one's self-will is broken; God's Will alone prevails, because only what He Wills has the power to be. In the presence of the transcendent Infinite, all that can be desired lies beyond, and draws us beyond, all that can be seen or known in the realm of formal existence. The practice, then, is to recognize *fear* as the presence of the truth that only God exists, and submit to being annihilated; to recognize *hurt* as the presence of the truth that God exceeds and violates all one's expectations, and allow oneself to be passively moved in accordance with His Will, 'like a corpse in the hands of a washer of the dead'; to recognize *anger* as God's command to us to cut the throat of self-will, instantly, and stand in wait for the dawning of God's Will, equally ready to actively cooperate with it, or to renounce action entirely if that be His wish; and to recognize *sadness* as a call from God to let what is dying in us die completely, and to rest, undying, in the depths of the Divine Nature, renouncing all longing for future solace and accepting instead the influx of present Mercy, in the realization that, while *all is perishing except His Face,* nonetheless *Wherever you turn, there is the face of God.*

Due to these correspondences with the metaphysical order, any feelings which go to feed remembrance instead of distracting one from it may be progressively transmuted into, or unveiled as, objective realities which transcend the subjective psyche, while functioning at the same time as the elements which compose that (apparent) psyche; these transpersonal feeling-tones are the reflection, on the affective level of the psychic plane, of the Names or Attributes of God. I would say—though God and the Sufis know best—that this is how feelings are experienced on the level of the spiritual Heart, which is not, as is often believed, the seat of subjective emotional reactions, but rather the site where objective Divine realities are witnessed. And the quintessence of these four elements, the mother of these transpersonal feeling-energies, is Love—the direct reflection, at the center of the psyche, of the objective Love of God. Again in Sufi terminology, I would tentatively identify this level of objective Love with the Spirit (*Ruh*), which is both Divine Love and the Universal Intellect, with absolutely no distinction between them.

When 'negative' emotions are recognized as the veiled faces of Love, they are transmuted into avenues leading to Love's realization. Conscious *anger* is the defense of Love against all that would violate it. Conscious sadness—*dard* in Persian—is the longing for the

(apparently) absent Beloved. Conscious *hurt* is the ability to wel-
come the 'unfairness' of the Beloved, all the plotting, the teasing,
and the slaps. And Conscious *fear* is the clear recognition, and full
acceptance, that end of True Love is Death. Thus the four classic elements of *romantic* love, spiritually transmuted, stand as the four
pillars of the throne of Divine Love.

When this is recognized, the second two of Schuon's stations of
wisdom have been accomplished: the peace of intimacy with Divine
Beauty, and the fervor which, by means of the attraction of manifest
Beauty—Paradise—hurls one toward union with the Invisible
Beauty—*Layla*, the Divine Essence. According to the *hadith*, 'God is
beautiful, and loves beauty.' That 'God is beautiful' is the archetype of
peace; that He 'loves beauty' is the archetype of fervor. God's nature
is Beauty, and whatever is beautiful is intrinsically lovable; this is why
the Sufis most often call Him 'the Beloved' and not 'the Lover'. Peace
and Beauty are intrinsically of God; fervent love of Beauty is
intrinsically of man. Yet God also 'loves Beauty'; this Love is His act of
Self-witnessing. And in the identical way, God loves man. In the
Qur'an (20:39–40) God says to Moses, *And I loaded on thee love from
me, and to be formed in My sight.* Moses, here, stands for the Human
Form, the *insan al-kamil*, which is formed and created, as Love, by
God's act of witnessing His own Essence. *God loves man because
God's rapture before His own Beauty is the essence of man.*

This rapture of Divine Self-regard is the first archetype and final
end of all human emotion. Therefore, as human emotion is alchemized, the obstacles become the Path. In the words of al-Hallaj, 'The
gnostic's ladder is his *nafs*. His essence is the gateway to Union with
God's Essence.' (Nurbakhsh, 1992, p 47)

Metaphysically, the truth that 'the obstacles are the Path' is based
on the nature of God as both transcendent and immanent: in the
words of the Qur'an, *all is perishing except His Face*, and yet *wherever
you turn, there is the face of God.* These are the last two of Schuon's
six stations of wisdom: *all is perishing* posits discrimination between
the Real and the unreal; *wherever you turn* posits identification and
union with the Real. Given that God is transcendent and unknowable, He is realized only by *fana*—by the letting go of the perishing,
contingent self and the world it perceives, till nothing but Allah

remains. Yet the other side of *fana* is *baqa*. The duality of subject-and-object, based on our false sense of self-existence, is annihilated in *fana*—but in *baqa*, it 'returns'—it appears in the realm of form, though understood to be unreal in the realm of essence. Where once it was a veil over Reality, it is now a manifestation of Reality. What were once the obstacles to the realization of the Divine are revealed as aspects of the Divine—and since this revelation, because it is objectively true whether or not we ever experience it, is virtual from the very beginning, the obstacles can indeed become the Path.

But the principle that 'the obstacles become the Path' must not be confused, as it too often is, with the antinomian tendency which preaches that it is only through sin that one can become holy, since God is beyond good and evil, that the way to avoid existential anxiety and painful self-division is to make common cause with the commanding *nafs*, and obey its every whim. The divinely-revealed *shari'ah* of Islam stands as a solid bulwark against that particular form of self-oppression. The practice of taking the obstacles as the Path is not a way of shirking the greater *jihad* against the *nafs-al-ammara*, but is in fact the very center of this *jihad* at its point of greatest intensity—comparable, in terms of the lesser *jihad*, to hand-to-hand combat.

Hard, painful emotions are a lot closer to True Love than is the intoxication of the self-satisfied *nafs*, no matter how deft it has become at reflecting metaphysical realities in order to avoid being transformed by them. To face such feelings directly is to practice spiritual poverty, *fakr*, in its most concrete form. When intolerable feelings arise, and the power to avoid them is nowhere to be seen, then God is our only refuge. In the words of Dr. Nurbakhsh, 'One who possesses such spiritual poverty is referred to as 'an impover-ished one' (*fakir*). Spiritual poverty is a state born of a sense of need, giving rise to the search for a remedy' (Nurbakhsh, 1979, p14).

One consequence of such spiritual poverty is that we will not make the mistake of thinking that we can fight the *nafs* with our own self-will; not only is our willfulness too weak a weapon to over-come the enemy, it is in fact an aspect of that same enemy. This is what Jesus was alluding to when, in reply to those who accused him of casting out devils by the Devil's own power, he answered that the

Devil would never consent to perform an exorcism because 'a house divided against itself cannot stand.' Our responsibility is to be present to the Presence of God, and let That One take the field against the rebellious *nafs* on His Own initiative, no matter how much suffering this might entail. This is the meaning of the Qur'anic verse, *You did not slay them, but God slew them; and when thou threwest, it was not thyself that threw, but God threw* (8:15), alluding to the moment, at the battle of Badr, when the prophet Muhammad (peace and blessings be upon him) threw a handful of pebbles at the enemy, after which the tide of battle turned. The same idea is expressed in a poem of Maghrebi:

> *No one can journey toward God on his own feet;*
> *To arrive at God's district, one must go with God's feet.*
> [Javad Nurbakhsh, *Discourses on the Sufi Path*, 1996, p 34]

The essence of spiritual combat is succinctly expressed in the 41st chapter of the Book of Job, verses 1–10, King James Version:

> Canst thou draw out Leviathan with a hook? Or his tongue with a cord which thou lettest down?
>
> Canst thou put a hook into his nose? Or bore his jaw through with a thorn?
>
> Will he make many supplications unto thee? Will he speak soft words to thee?
>
> Will he make a covenant with thee? Wilt thou take him for a servant forever?
>
> Wilt thou play with him as with a bird? Or wilt thou bind him for thy maidens?
>
> Shall the companions make a banquet of him? Shall they part him among the merchants?
>
> Canst thou fill his skull with barbed irons? Or his head with fish spears?
>
> Lay thine hand upon him, remember the battle, do no more.
>
> Behold, the hope of him is in vain: shall not one be cast down, even at the sight of him?
>
> None is so fierce that dare stir *him* up: who then is able to stand before *Me*?

Leviathan, the sea-monster, is obviously the *nafs al-ammara*. God here is denying, or actually satirizing, the foolish and arrogant idea that the instinctual powers of the psyche are ours to use however we will, that we can control them with ease because they are 'who we really are'. To 'play with him as with a bird' is to believe that we can control our own thoughts simply by deciding to, while to 'bind him for thy maidens' to 'make a banquet of him' and to 'part him among the merchants' refer to the equally foolish belief that lust, gluttony and greed can be controlled in the same way. 'None is so fierce that dare stir *him* up: who then is able to stand before *Me*?' means that God alone has the power to subdue Leviathan. Our sole duty in the war between God and the great sea-monster is to 'lay thine hand upon him'—that is, not to repress or deny the *nafs al-ammara* but simply to stay 'in touch' with it, while in every other sense *getting out of the way* so that God Himself can subdue it. To 'remember the battle' is to remember that only God fights this battle and only He can win it; it is also and equally to understand that the remembrance of God *is* the battle, and that constancy in this remembrance is entirely our own responsibility. The power to subdue and pacify the *nafs* is God's alone; our part is simply to *be the channel* by which the power of God can come to grips with it. Thus the ultimate weapon in spiritual combat is, precisely, the act of attention, which in spiritual terms, as an established level of being, is none other than *al-Qalb*, the spiritual Heart.

The relationship between 'self-power' and 'other-power' on the field of spiritual combat is concisely rendered in these terms by Frithjof Schuon, in the last paragraph of *Stations of Wisdom*:

All great spiritual experiences agree in this: that there is no common measure between the means put into operation and the result. 'With men this is impossible, but with God all things are possible,' says the Gospel. In fact, what separates man from divine Reality is the slightest of barriers: God is infinitely close to man, but man is infinitely far from God. This barrier, for man, is a mountain; man must stand in front of a mountain which he must remove with his own hands. He digs away the earth, but in vain, the mountain remains; man however goes on digging, in the name of God. And the mountain vanishes. It was never there [Schuon, 1961, p 157].

## REFERENCES

Feng, Gia Fu and English, Jane (1972), *Tao Te Ching* (New York: Vintage Books).

Ibn al-'Arabi (1980), *The Bezels of Wisdom*, New York: Paulist Press. Translated by R.W.J. Austin. From the chapter 'The Wisdom of Expiration in the Word of Seth'.

Kelley, C.F. (1977), *Meister Eckhart on Divine Knowledge*, New Haven: Yale University Press.

Lings, Martin. (1987), *The Eleventh Hour: The Spiritual Crisis of the Modern World in the Light of Tradition and Prophesy*, Cambridge: Quinta Essentia.

Nasr, Seyyed Hossein. (1978), *An Introduction to Islamic Cosmological Doctrines*, Boulder: Shambhala.

Nurbakhsh, Javad. (1978), *In the Tavern of Ruin: Seven Essays on Sufism*, New York: Khaniqahi-Nimatullahi Publications.

_____(1979) *In the Paradise of the Sufis*, New York: Khaniqahi-Nimatullahi Publications

_____(1981), *Sufism: Meaning, Knowledge and Unity*, New York: Khaniqahi-Nimatullahi Publications

_____(1985) *Sufism III*, London: Khaniqahi-Nimatullahi Publications

_____(1992), *The Psychology of Sufism*, London, New York: Khaniqahi-Nimatullahi Publications

_____(1996), *Discourses on the Sufi Path*, London, New York: Khaniqahi-Nimatullahi Publications

Schuon, Frithjof. (1954), *Spiritual Perspectives and Human Facts*. London: Faber & Faber.

_____(1961), *Stations of Wisdom*, Bedfont: Perennial Books.

_____(1986), *Survey of Metaphysics and Esoterism*, Bloomington: World Wisdom Books.

_____(1991), *Roots of the Human Condition*, Bloomington: World Wisdom Books.

# VI

## FACETS

Why is it that those dark-eyed, statuesque beauties
With faces like the full moon
Never wear the color
Of constancy?

There is no defect in your beauty, except this one:
That the loveliness of that face can never be divided
Between love, and constancy.

[*after Hafiz*]

# THE PEOPLE OF BLAME

IN CHRISTIANITY there are those who are called 'fools for Christ', such as St. Basil, who ate raw meat in front of Ivan the Terrible during the Lenten fast and invited the Czar to join him, because he was, in effect, already eating the people of Russia alive, and St. Xenia of Petersburg, a 'mentally ill' homeless woman who endured the Russian winter with neither shelter nor fire, was clairvoyant, and performed miracles. In Sufism, such people are called the *Malamatiyya*, the 'people of blame'. Some Sufi masters, such as Ibn al-'Arabi, name the people of blame as the highest of all among the friends of God. (In the Lakota religion, such people are referred to as the *Heyoka*—though the Lakota understand them not as simply mentally ill or socially maladjusted, but as sacred clowns, both humorous and terrifying, as people dominated by the Name of God 'the Thunderbird'.)

Ibn al-'Arabi, with a touch of irony, describes the people of blame as those who have transcended the level of flamboyant spiritual ecstasy, and settled down in simple self-annihilation to the degree that they seem—like Kierkegaard's 'knight of faith'—to be no different than the general run of believers. But both the people of blame and the fools for Christ are most often defined as those who appear as mad, as socially inept, or even as flagrant sinners to most of their fellow worshippers.

It is said that the people of blame choose to appear crazy or wicked to others in order to mortify their own social vanity—and perhaps secondarily, like Lear's fool, to call into question the collective vanity of the society around them. It is very difficult for us, however, to imagine how a simple case of social rambunctiousness could be in any way a mortification of vanity, since our culture teaches us that the *right kind* of anti-social behavior—the socially acceptable kind—is vanity's chosen paradise. Sometimes (in Hollywood, at least) it can even make you rich. The hippies, for example, loved nothing better than 'freaking out the straights', ostensibly for the purpose of helping them see beyond the limitations of their unquestioned social mores, but in reality (at least in most cases) to feed the social vanity of the hippies themselves.

The roving dervish or troubadour dressed in gay colors, the sly merry trickster, the foolish happy clown—these are the images through which self-styled American 'holy fools' most often view the quality and destiny of the People of Blame. But, of course, it's not that simple—because blame hurts. It's not so easy to rise above the blame laid on us by our society, especially when it is laid by those with a degree of true spiritual virtue.

Jesus Himself, of course, was a holy fool—but we can't easily see this. Images of Him calmly and nobly casting the money changers out of the Temple or heart-rendingly praying on the Mount of Olives have blinded us to the fact that the cross was not only an instrument of torture and execution, but also an emblem of shame. The good, pious Jews, even members of his own family, were ashamed of his antics, and even doubted his sanity: he 'went ballistic' in the Temple itself! And if He was true man as well as true God, if He was as fully human as you or me, do you think He himself was never ashamed of His own behavior? Of course He was. If He had not endured feelings shame and degradation as well as physical and mental torture, His grace would never have been able to penetrate to those, like the prostitutes and slaves and tax collectors, who lived their daily lives under social shame and obloquy. The Prophet Muhammad, peace and blessings be upon him, felt similar shame when members of his own family rejected him, when the revelations of the Qur'an stopped for a time, and when he, a prophet of God with all God's power behind him, lost an important battle. Many of the *surahs* of the Qur'an are filled with exhortations from God that he not lose faith in his mission or knuckle under to the disbelief and slander heaped upon him by Meccan society. And the famous Sufi Mansur al-Hallaj revealed the mysteries of *tasawwuf* to the uninitiated and even claimed to be God (apparently, and in a certain sense), in what could be considered the most foolish and blameworthy manner, since he was martyred because if it. In his prayer delivered on the scaffold, he forgave his executioners just as

Christ did, excusing them by saying:

> Those who adore thee, O God, have assembled here to kill me
> out of their love for You, so that they may come closer to You.
> Pardon them, O Lord! If You had revealed to them what You
> revealed to me, they would not have done what they have done;
> and if You had concealed from me what You concealed from
> them, I would not have suffered this tribulation. Power and
> glory be to You in whatever You do, and power and glory be to
> You in whatever You will.

The Old Testament is filled with stories of prophets, such as
Jonah, who would have tried anything to escape their calling: rather
be swallowed by a great fish and sunk in the depths of the sea than
follow God's hard command to preach to Nineveh. And it is no different with the People of Blame. St. Xenia only entered this exclusive circle after she went insane following her husband's death, and
ended up as what we would call a 'bag-lady'. And although Jean-
Claude Larchet makes it clear that the 'fool for Christ' is not simply
an impulsive madman who can't help himself, but one who adopts
that role consciously and deliberately, in a larger sense the initiate of
the People of Blame is dominated and abased by God for His Own
greater glory; if he knowingly chooses that path, it is only because
he understands that this is God's will for him, which he must obey
whether he likes it or not. No one, in other words, becomes a member of the *Malamatiyyia* by following his or her preferences; if so, he
or she is nothing but a self-appointed pseudo-prophet. And if the
one so abased by God can bring himself to accept the painful destiny laid upon him by the Almighty—with resignation, and ultimately with gratitude—then he will indeed be among the highest
and most intimate of all the friends of God. But not so fast, and not
so easy. We can't humble ourselves *in order to be* exalted—we can do
so only because God is tremendous in His might and power, and all
glory is due Him, and none can stand against Him. But if we have
the courage, the trust and the love not to run from His chastise-
ment, we will understand how abasement is inseparable from exaltation: if arrogance is abased, God is exalted—in us.

# THE SCALES

GOD IS THE LIGHT of the Heavens and the Earth, the First and the Last, the Inner and the Outer. The Inner, in essence, takes precedence over the Outer. But if the Inner is sought to the exclusion of the Outer, it flees, whereas if the Inner and the Outer are given equal weight on the scales, then the Inner takes precedence, because the Divine Reality embraces both Inner and Outer, and the Inner is the direct expression of that Reality.

If the Outer in religion is abandoned, then the world is abandoned to the commanding *nafs*. Daily, outer life becomes profane, and the soul is swept up in its profanity. The same thing happens if the Outer is granted precedence: without the life-giving breath of the Inner, religion itself becomes profane. But to establish the Outer while remembering the Inner is to invoke the presence of the Inner which, in this life, needs something in relation to which it can be Inner.

Those *batinis* (devotees of the Inner) who seek the Inner and find it are dominated by their state. One who is dominated by his state can inspire others, he can feed them with the milk of the Spirit. But for me to attain the state of another can never be a legitimate or possible aspiration. Unless I am Outer in relation to that Innerness, I can never reach the Inner. The Law makes me Outer; it particularizes me and individualizes me. It frees me from dominance by the state of the Guide, a state I can never attain; consequently I can be guided. It makes me small so I can aspire. It places me in the field of the magnetic attraction of the Lodestone of the Pole. It establishes me as Man by its universality, and as particular by my particular obedience to it. It leads me fully to my own destined station, no matter how modest, by freeing me from vicarious participation in the state of the Guide, no matter how exalted. That exaltation can never be mine. That stolen state is a barrier to my earned station; that longed-for state is a barrier to the unearned state that God gives me freely. This is why he true Guide is not a treasure, but a door.

# JESUS AND MUHAMMAD AS 'REVOLUTIONARIES'

*(From Correspondence)*

AFTER READING some of what your friend had to say, I was moved to reply to two points. One reply is simply a caution: A dedication of one's life to 'absolute Truth, Love and Justice' can be nothing less than a dedication of that life to the Absolute, to God Himself. Only in God are Truth, Love, and Justice absolute; in this relative world, Truth, Love, and Justice can only be attained in a relative manner, to a relative degree. On the material plane we must always be careful not to violate Truth in the act of proclaiming it, or Love in the act of establishing it, or Justice in the act of enforcing it. As Berthold Brecht said, in one of his poems: 'Ah, we who desired to prepare the soil for kindness/ Could not ourselves be kind'. This sentiment would have been much more moving and hopeful if Brecht had been followed by a generation or two of conspicuously kind Marxist-Leninists.

My second comment has to do with your friend's characterization of Jesus, peace and blessings be upon him, as a 'revolutionary'. This is something I used to believe when I identified with the Liberation Theology movement. At this point I am no longer comfortable with it. Jesus' ministry certainly had a profoundly revolutionary effect on society, but this does not mean that to designate him as a 'social revolutionary' is correct. He was a prophet. And unlike the Prophet Muhammad, peace and blessings be upon him, whose delegated role included (but was certainly not limited to) the direct expression of military and political power in a revolutionary manner, Jesus' influence was theurgic, spiritual and moral, not political. That political consequences flowed from that ministry in later centuries should not blind us to this rather obvious truth.

Liberation Theology sees the dispossessed classes of the world as the carriers of a prophetic mandate simply by virtue of their oppression. The 'poor' who shall 'see God' are not just the economically unlucky, however; if they were, anyone could achieve sainthood simply by losing all his or her money in the stock market. They are 'the poor in spirit', those who have lost their lives for God, and found their lives in Him. (The Arabic word *fuqara*, more or less synonymous with 'Sufis', has substantially the same meaning.) This false identification of material with spiritual poverty is one of the central errors of Liberation Theology. The materially poor can be just as eaten up by sullen, rebellious pride as the rich often are by cruel, oppressive pride—thus Jesus's teaching of 'love your enemies, do good to those who harm you.' Jesus did not identify himself exclusively with the cause of the materially oppressed. He ministered to Roman centurions, Pharisees and the hated tax collectors *as well as* to prostitutes, laborers and beggars. Though he was critical of the privileged sects and classes—the Scribes, Pharisees, Sadducees and Herodians—and silent with regard to the Zealots, the anti-Roman revolutionary terrorists, the point of his social critique was most often directed against those who perverted true religion, not against those holding political power. And his words to Peter on the occasion of his arrest, 'those who live by the sword shall die by the sword,' certainly reveal what must have been his fundamental attitude toward the Zealots. (Jesus' words applied to the Romans as well—some of whom were within earshot—especially since the Roman name for the capital punishment he was about to suffer at their hands was *ius gladii*, 'judgment by the sword'.) Jesus told the rich young man that his way to perfection was to give all he had to the poor, but he also required that the lepers 'give up' their leprosy, that the 5,000 give up their hunger and neediness, that Peter give up his faithlessness, that the attacked and offended give up their right to just retaliation. He was the enemy not of material riches per se, but of idolatry in all its forms. To Jesus, the common oppressors of both the materially rich and the materially poor were Sin and Death. It was these spiritual powers, not the worldly power of political or economic oppression, that he came to overthrow. It is true that his recognition of charity as the highest virtue did in fact ameliorate a vast amount of material suffering in the following centuries. But the paradigm he taught, and acted from, was not *rebellion against the oppressors*, but *compassion for the suffering*.

The clearest expression of the position Jesus assumed in relation to the political forces of his day appears in the story of the Roman coin. The Pharisees had publicly challenged him to answer this question: Is it lawful to pay the tax to Rome? If he answered 'yes', he would lose his following among the Zealots and their many supporters, since one of their doctrines was that, in light of the cult of Emperor-worship that had been instituted in some of the Roman provinces, to pay the tax to Caesar was *literally* an act of idolatry—especially since the Emperor's image appeared on the coin the tax was to be paid with, which, to the traditionally an-iconic Jews, would inevitably suggest a pagan idol. (Muslims share the same traditional suspicion of images, particularly images of the Divinity.) And if he answered 'no', he would have been arrested for sedition on the spot. So they thought they had him. How he escaped this trap was a masterpiece of spiritual and political 'street theatre'. First, he asked if anyone present had a Roman coin, thereby demonstrating that he and his followers *did not*; they were of the poor. When handed one, he asked: 'Whose image is this?' The answer, of course, was 'Caesar's'—not 'God's.' 'Render therefore unto Caesar what is Caesar's, and to God what is God's' he answered, by which he meant: 'Anyone who thinks that this is an image of God is an idolator. It is only the image of a man. There is no idolatry in paying the tax, therefore; the Roman state is not God. What we owe to God is immensely more precious than money: He requires of us a "contrite heart", not "the fat of rams"'. (We can see here how this position was perfectly in line with his act of driving the money-changers out of the Temple.) So Jesus was able to criticize the Zealots' idea of the 'spiritual' significance of the Roman tax, but in such a way that he was in fact far more critical of Rome, and more accurately so, than even they were. And at the same time he avoided limiting his ministry to a simple rebellion against the worldly powers that be; if he had been arrested and executed as a mere preacher against taxation, the significance of his self-sacrifice as it ultimately transpired would never have been revealed.

As for your friend's characterization of the Prophet Muhammad, peace and blessings be upon him, as a social revolutionary, this was certainly *part* of his mission. We must be very careful, however, not to confuse the social aspects of a divine revelation brought by a prophet with those revolutions initiated by secular, western revolutionaries and ideologues; the gulf between them is immense, however much the modern Islamicists, in their jealous, imitative hatred of the west, have forgotten it.

# QIYAMAT
# AL-QIYAMAT

*For Ali Lakhani*

THE UNIVERSE is born and dies in the rhythm of the breath. The phase of inhalation relates to creation, both as an act of God and as the universe of created things: all the Names of God fully deployed as the cosmos, and also unified and synthesized as the Creator, whose locus-of-manifestation is the Human Form. As God exhales the Mercy of Existence, creation breathes it in.

The phase of exhalation relates to the Divine Essence, and the return of all things to that Essence. As God exhales the universe into being, man inhales the Breath of the Merciful, and is created thereby as the Primordial Adam, *Adam awwal kulli*, the epitome of all the Names. As man exhales the universe, thereby releasing it from the Seal of Universal Existence which is the Human Form, God draws the subtle essences of all things back into His breast, unites them with His Heart, and hides them in His Essence. Nothing that is not first created can return to its Source; by creating all things, the Creator allows for the return of all things to His own Essence. The Creator is on the path *of al-Rahman*; The Essence is reached by the path of *al-Rahim*. The Creator casts the net; the Essence hauls it in. The Creator is *Am I not your Lord?* to which all things answer *Yea!* And the Essence is: 'Die before you die,' which is also to say: In Essence you are annihilated already.

And from the standpoint of the Reality, which encompasses both Creator/creation and Essence with no polarity between them, these two motions are simultaneous; the Reality is the Sun orbited by the single motion of creation-and-return, just as, in the human body, the breath orbits the Heart.

The dead are those who cannot die. They lie in their tombs alive, tossing in nightmare. Whatever is repressed in my psyche, whatever is not liberated from its tomb, whatever is not allowed to die, fuels the passions of the *nafs al-ammara*. It enters the world of the living dead, of those who have been denied the resurrection by their very struggle to rise.

When the breath leaves the body, when the universe is exhaled, the general resurrection is accomplished: the dead of all places and times, both past and future, rise through me, in a great column of light. The *nafs al-ammara* believes that it fights for all the wronged and insulted dead; it thinks that, fuelled by their anger, it only struggles in their cause. All the blood it sheds, its own and that of its enemies, is shed in the name of the martyrs of Karbala.

But the fiery anger of the *nafs al-ammara* does not liberate the dead, but only imprisons them; it locks them in the tombs. The anger of the dead that feeds the fire of the *nafs al-ammara* is not the desire of the dead for revenge on their enemies, as the *nafs al-ammara* likes to believe, but is actually the anger of the dead at the *nafs al-ammara* itself, the fiery warrior who imprisons them. It is the anger of those whom anger has deprived of freedom; it is their anger against anger itself.

But when I die before I die, when I exhale the universe of forms back to the Essence, then I am host to the Last Imam, to *al-Qaim*; the general resurrection takes place; the dead of all places and times arise. Instead of claiming to fight for them, I die to release them; they ascend in the Pillar of Light, *al-amud an-Nur*, back to the Heart of the Essence. Could I die for myself alone? Who would die voluntarily, unless he knew that by that dying he had the power to save? Who could give up war unless he knew that in doing so he would accomplish the aim of war, which is peace—unless he realized that there is in fact no other way to accomplish it—unless he understood that the only value in fighting is to demonstrate that fighting is in no way greater than dying, that dying is actually greater than fighting—and that he who dies perfectly, at the first breath, at the first sigh, need never draw his sword?

*O Shi'a! Warriors of God!*
*You who remember the martyrdom of Hussein*
*And the suppression of the True Line:*
*Seek the Twelfth Imam*
*Not at noon, but at midnight;*
*When you find the Hidden One*
*It will be in the Hidden Place.*

# SUFI MANIFESTO

THERE IS nothing essential in Sufi doctrine that is not ultimately a commentary on the Noble Qur'an and the prophetic *ahadith*—the flawed scholarship of the orientalists and the fantasies of the anti-traditional pseudo-esoterics notwithstanding. Those so-called Sufis who try to separate Sufism from Islam, no matter how sincere they may be, are like cut flowers in a vase. Until the water that sustains them evaporates, they bloom and give off fragrance—but in reality they possess only the semblance of life, and the power to reproduce is forever denied them. God in His Mercy may save them in view of their sincerity, because He has the power to save whoever He will—but the norms He Himself has laid down for the soul's return to Him will form no part of that saving act. To reject the religion brought by Muhammad, peace and blessings be upon him, is to cut the *silsila* that stretches back to him, and from him to Gabriel, and from Gabriel to Allah—to deprive it of all meaning, and of any effectiveness except (perhaps) a temporary and fading one.

Sufism is not a revelation in itself—a truth that some Sufis may lose sight of in view of the fact that the basic practices and some of the lore of *tasawwuf* clearly pre-date Islam. The Christian practice of the Prayer of the Heart, referred to in several places in the New Testament, as when St. Paul recommends that we 'pray without ceasing,' or when St. Peter speaks of the moment when 'the day-star shall arise in your hearts,' is almost identical in form to the Sufi *dhikr*. Certain indications in the Old Testament also appear to refer to the practice of the invocation of God's Name, such as passages from the Psalms like 'our heart will rejoice in Him because we have trusted in His Holy Name' [33:21] and 'unite my heart to fear Thy Name' [86:11]. And certainly some Sufi lore and practices came into the tradition from pre-Islamic Central Asia. The question is: Did lore and practice from the ancient Near East and Central Asia enter Islam so as to become part of Sufism? Or did Sufism depart from

Islam to seek that lore and practice in foreign lands and religions? The answer is obvious: the pre-Islamic and non-Islamic lore and spiritual practices were the guests, but Islam was the host. And it is the host who provides the nourishment. To say that Sufism is not intrinsically Islamic is no different from saying that the Tibetans who practice the Vajrayana are not really Buddhists, since many of their practices ultimately derived from the shamanic religion of Bön. Certainly they drew upon Bön, but whatever entered Buddhism from that religion became *essentially* Buddhist, not just accidentally so. No spiritual lore or practice is spiritually effective unless it sits at the table of one of God's great revelations to humanity; to attempt to carry on such practice outside one of these revelations is to turn it over to the self-will of the ego, to the *nafs al-ammara*. As every Sufi *silsila* attests, living contact with God's *baraka* comes through His revelation to humanity in the Noble Qur'an and the way of the Prophet Muhammad, peace and blessings be upon him; every special unveiling or grace given and received in the course of spiritual practice and attainment, even in the case of the greatest Sufi masters, is only effective in that context. It may seem as if the existence of spiritual seekers and masters who reached high stations outside, or between, the great revelations—such as Waraqah the Hanif or Uways al-Qarani—proves that such revelations are unnecessary and can be ignored with impunity. Such is not the case. Waraqah was a Christian, and was waiting for the new revelation destined to come through Muhammad, which he gladly embraced. And although Uways al-Qarani, who is sometimes given as an example of a 'Sufi' master outside Islam, never met the Prophet, he did embrace Islam when news of it came to him; this is undoubtedly what Muhammad meant when he said, referring to Uways, 'I feel the Breath of the Merciful coming to me from the Yemen.' When God opens a clear path, and we still foolishly think we can invent our own path or find a better one, then God help us.

Many Sufis who emigrate from nations with oppressive Islamicist regimes go to pieces in the comparative religious freedom of the west. They are so relieved not to be under the thumb of the Wahhabis, the Ayatollahs, the religious police that they gladly dump the *shari'ah*, even the Five Pillars, and revel in their new-found liberty. It is one thing to abbreviate the shari'ah, sometimes radically, so as to make it possible to practice it in a balanced way in non-Islamic nations; it is quite another thing to abandon it entirely. I cannot think of a single historical example where an esoterism such as *tasawwuf* deserted its parent religion without eventually—or immediately—turning into a heterodox cult, a political cadre, a universalist pseudo-religion, or all three at once. And though it is understandable that some Sufis in the west would want to publicly distance themselves from Islam— particularly after 9/11—the fact remains that the persecution faced by Muslims in Western nations is nothing compared to the persecution faced by Sufis in certain Islamic nations. Whether or not they openly admit it, some Sufis who immigrate to the West feel relieved to be 'freed' from Islam itself, forgetting that they *are* Islam, that as traditional Sufis they are much more truly Islamic than the Islamicists ever could be. What they don't seem to realize is that in drifting aimlessly away from Islam over the seas of western secularism, they are actually obeying the orders of the Wahhabis, the Ayatollahs, the religious police. Those heartless oppressors would like see Sufism ejected from Islam entirely—and those westernized Sufis who separate Sufism from its Islamic roots are blithely and unwittingly doing their work for them. The Islamicists slander Sufism by calling it heterodox and anti-Islamic, and then the westernized Sufis prove them right by transforming themselves into the very image of the heterodox, non-Islamic Sufi, perfectly validating the Islamicist ideology upon whose false image of Sufism they have patterned themselves. Westernized Sufis sometimes justify dumping the *shari'ah* by pointing to the all-too-common example of those Muslims who become obsessed with it, who use the law as a whip against others rather applying it to themselves in an attempt to become true human beings. But whether the ego of the exoteric Muslim obsessed with the law or that of the so-called Sufi who prides himself on being above the law is the hungrier beast, God only knows.

The Sufis of the west should stand against the Islamicists, not obey them. They should not abandon Islam to the Wahhabis and the other anti-Sufi Muslims, but should claim it for their own. This need not be done in a politicized or 'activist' way, with public demonstrations and denunciations; all that is required is that western Sufis should stand in the tradition of their own great exemplars of the past, in the lineage stretching back to the first Sufis, in the days when Sufism was a reality without a name, not a name without a reality— to Ali ibn Abi Talib and the Prophet Muhammad himself, peace and blessings be upon them. It is in the west alone that they are almost entirely free to do this; it would be a tragedy if they did not fully avail themselves of that freedom, while it still exists.

If there is one thing that immigrants to the west from dar al-Islam need to understand—something that under present conditions it is very difficult for them to get a clear picture of—it is the history of the West's religious opposition to its own secularization, and of the relentless ejection of religious doctrines and values from the arena of public discourse. They do not realize that religious freedom, which is a good thing in itself and a necessary aspect of any humane, religiously-pluralistic society, is inseparable in practical terms from a militant secularism that devalues *all* religion, relegating it to the 'private' realm alone—and that religious freedom in the west has already begun to be seriously curtailed by the very 'democratic' secularism that brought it into being. To the degree that Sufis abandon their Islamic roots, and are content to occupy only the shapeless 'interfaith' zone designed by the secular globalists as a sort of theme-park to keep the traditional religions pacified, subject to a false sense of security calculated to blind them to their increasing marginalization under the 'oppressive tolerance' of the west, they will not be able to stand together in any effective way, either vocally or silently, with their brothers and sisters of the other world religions, against the forces of militant secularism and official denial of God that menace them all.

Sleepers, awake.

When I saw the beauty of your face
Suddenly I understood the meaning of a verse
    of the Qur'an
That had long eluded me:
Ever since that night, grace and beauty
Have been the whole of my exegesis.

[*after Hafiz*]

# VII
## HISTORIES

# FIVE PROPHETS

*In Light of the* Fusus al-Hikam

### ABRAHAM

If you were not my Secret,
How could I ever have found you,
Among the tents?
If I were not your own Secret, jealously guarded,
How could I ever have submitted
To being called Your friend?
When I knew myself alone,
Exiled from the world,
I discovered your secret Name
Inscribed on the Guarded Tablet.
When I emerged from that solitude,
To lose myself in tribes and armies,
You felt my loss.
You searched for me everywhere,
Found me in my exile,
And named me Your friend.
At Your command I raised my right hand
To kill my son;
I looked again, and he was Thou:
I dropped the knife.
When we sat together on a cushion of grass
Inside the Walled Garden of the Mysteries,
Eating from our vine and fig tree
And talking to our heart's content,
The desert, shimmering white and yellow
On the horizon beyond us
Stood in need of the clear Arabic tongue.

In love you led me
Into the barren places of the earth.
In anger you drove me, with slaps and bitter words
Toward the chamber of Night
Where you were waiting for me already,
Watching over my sleep,
The rising and falling of my breast,
Till the mazes of the stars and the night of time
Passed over, and the morning came.

### NOAH AND ADAM

The Prophet Noah overthrew the idols:
Grotesque statues with the heads of animals.
The sea of space and time closed over them.
Noah rode the flood
On the Ark of the Human Form,
Surrounded by all the animals, two by two,
In Beauty and Majesty;
And the ribs of the Prophet Adam
Were the timbers of that ship.
Before sun and moon and stars were made,
Adam, by God's command,
Recited the Names
Of the beasts and their angels.
As the generations rose,
Hunting beasts for meat and
Naming them for power,
God sent the Prophet Noah to remind us
That no beast possesses his own name
Or knows how to speak it.
When the forms of other-than-God
Are drowned in the flood,
Then the Names of God are gathered,
And Man—hidden form of the Formless
Secret word of the Silence—
Is their Book and their Ark.

## MOSES COMPLAINS OF TORAH

Her generosity to many was her wrath;
    her cruelty to me, her mercy.
Though she played the Pharaoh
    in the tyranny of her beauty,
She required me to be Moses,
    and walk the narrow path.

—

[If Moses had come down from Sinai without Torah,
He would have burned to ashes the Children of Israel.]


## SALIH

The prophet Salih bought a she-camel from
    God—
The Tribe of Thamud hamstrung it.
But didn't both tribe and camel drink from
    the same well?
The Tribe of Thamud feasted for three days
Until God's Shout destroyed them in their
    tents.
But wasn't Salih the one who led that camel
    to slaughter in the first place?
And were the Tribe of Thamud liable to God's
    judgment
Before the prophet Salih broke in upon their
    sleep?
If the elements had not risen up against God
    He could never have created them; by His
    world-creating Shout
He destroyed them in their rebellious non-entity,
And sent them out, His willing slaves, into the
    mountains and deserts of this world.
*Whatever departs from God*, said the prophet
    Salih
*Is most surely on its way to Him.*

# THE TALE OF THE FAQIR
# WITH THE GOLDEN CLOAK

ONCE UPON A TIME there was a wandering faqir who possessed—somehow—a magnificent golden cloak, embroidered with precious gems. Wherever he went he wore the same shining garment; and, since his circle of wandering was actually quite small, soon he was known far and wide, to the people he met, as The Faqir with the Golden Cloak.

One day, while traveling along the highroad, singing a little song to himself in praise of the free life of God's poor, he encountered a band of robbers. 'Oho!' they cried. 'If the life of holy poverty is indeed such a free one, let us make haste to liberate this servant of Allah from his cloak of gold.' 'Stand back!' warned the faqir. 'This cloak is a gift of God, and those who steal God's gifts will surely incur His wrath.' 'We'll take that chance,' laughed the robbers, and after raining on him a storm of kicks and blows for his trouble, stripped him of his Golden Cloak and rode off.

Bruised and crestfallen, the faqir continued on his way down the highroad, none too sure—if the truth be known—that the God's wrath would necessarily fall upon his adversaries any time soon; after all, *he* was the one with all the bruises, wasn't he? Still, he commended himself to Allah, and walked on. Imagine his surprise, then, when he turned a corner in the road, and saw before him the robbers who had just waylaid him, lying dead in a pool of their own blood. At first he could not understand what had happened; but then he looked up, and saw the Golden Cloak hung on a tree of thorns, beneath which lay the corpses of the robbers. Slowly it dawned upon him that the robbers had in fact killed one another. They had been fighting for possession of the cloak, which, they realized, would lose half its value if they divided it. 'Praise be to Allah!' cried the faqir. 'This goes to prove how generous He is, and how just in His dealings with His servants. He has simply been testing me, that much is certain.' Then the delighted dervish wrapped himself anew in his Golden Cloak, which—if the truth be known—he'd been certain that he would never see again. 'How great is Allah! He has punished my enemies and returned to me what is rightfully mine, however undeserved.' And the faqir continued on his journey with a light heart.

A few days later, the faqir crossed over into a kingdom and down into a valley which was being invaded by an enemy king. Galloping knights, thronging cavalry, and the shout and clash of battle where everywhere. In the course of the battle the faqir was taken prisoner by the soldiers of the invading king, and within a few short days found himself incarcerated in the king's fortress. However, he was kept in decent quarters, and even allowed audiences with the king, who respected dervishes even while keeping them prisoner. He even allowed the faqir to keep his cloak—'for,' said the king, 'I am a rich man, and it would not be appropriate for me to possess the cloak of one of God's poor, no matter how valuable it appears.'

The faqir thought himself lucky, all-in-all. His host was certainly more generous than he, a prisoner, had any right to expect. Still, he was not happy. He began to experience great loneliness, and pined for his family and friends. Eventually, the king noticed his distress. 'Why are you so sad, my friend?' asked the king. 'Is my court not to your liking? Is there something else you desire in life than to be my servant, which is *my* desire?' 'O King,' said Ibrahim—for that was the faqir's name—'your bounty and generosity are without flaw; still, I cannot be happy as a prisoner in your court. I long to see my wife and family; who knows what is happening to them without me?' 'Very well,' said the king, 'I can certainly understand your great attachment to your loved ones. But I cannot simply let you go; I took you in war, and you are fair spoil. However, you may ransom yourself if you can. Have you no friends willing to pay your price, no property you can turn into ready cash? Why not this cloak of yours? The price of it in silver would be more than enough to buy your freedom.' Ibrahim pondered the king's offer, and—after a struggle with his conscience—he offered to send the cloak to his family with one of the king's messengers, with instructions to sell it, and ransom him with the proceeds.

Than night the messenger departed, and as dawn was breaking, he arrived at the house of Ibrahim's wife and family. When his cousins saw the Golden Cloak, and heard from the messenger the tale of Ibrahim's captivity and the king's demand for ransom, they hurried to the market, and sold the cloak for (they feared) considerably less than it was worth. But it was enough and more than enough to meet the king's demand, and that night the messenger who has brought the cloak set out with an ass-load of silver toward the king's fortress. He arrived at dawn. When the king saw the ransom paid, he summoned the faqir and dismissed him with blessings, but also with regret. 'I am sorry that you found our court not to your liking,' he said. 'Still, I hope you will remember your stay here with us, and sometimes think of us; certainly we will remember you.' Promising to remember, Ibrahim bowed, and left the court of the king.

So the faqir started off on his long way home. He traveled slowly, with many stops and detours, in great weariness; even the prospect of being reunited with his family could not overcome his feeling of desolation. The truth was, he felt out of place, meaningless and vulnerable, to be traveling through the world without his Golden Cloak. 'I have not encountered one person on this journey who has greeted me by name; no one recognizes me without my Golden Cloak. If the truth be known, I hardly recognize myself.' At last he came to the outskirts of the town where his family lived; slowly he made his way through the streets to the door of his home—but when he tried to enter, the inmates raised a cry. 'Who are you, insolent beggar, to be breaking into honest people's houses? By off with you before we call the constable!' 'Don't you recognize me?' cried the faqir. 'I am your cousin Ibrahim.' 'Ibrahim!' they retorted. 'Ibrahim has been rotting in prison for years now, and you are not he! Your face is unfamiliar to us. Be off!' Sadly, Ibrahim turned back the way he had come. So it was true! Not even his own family recognized him without his Golden Cloak.

From that day forward, Ibrahim became a homeless wanderer, through a world that no longer recognized him, and which was unfamiliar to him as well. No glad voices hailed him. He wandered from land to land, without prospects, without identity, with neither goal nor hope of attaining it. Years went by.

One night, in a far country, Ibrahim found himself sitting beside a meager fire of dry thorn bushes, at a wayside camping spot by the highroad. As he sat and shivered, he heard the sound of travelers approaching, accompanied by piercing wails of anguish. Startled, Ibrahim concealed himself behind some bushes, and watched. Soon, into the circle of the firelight, a funeral procession emerged, with bearers carrying the corpse in a screened litter. As they stopped and lay down their burden by the fire, a woman—obviously the bereaved widow—threw herself to the ground in a paroxysm of grief. Ibrahim was perplexed, and uncertain how to respond. Years of lonely travel had made him wary, and the sight of the husky bearers and attendants reminded him only too clearly of past beatings. But as the woman continued to moan and fling herself about, his heart softened. So he rose from his hiding place and timidly approached. 'I could not help being touched by your great grief,' he said to the widow. 'Is there anything I can do to lighten your burden?' 'Anything you can do!' cried the bereaved wife. 'As if you, or anyone, could do anything for me now! If you had only known my husband you would not have made such an offer, kindly meant as it was. He was the kindest, most wonderful man I have ever known.' And with that the woman launched into a long rambling tale, broken by sobs—the tale of her grief, of her life, of her love for her husband and the circumstances of his death. Ibrahim listened with a feeling of helplessness. How could someone bowed down with his own sorrows do anything to lighten the sorrows of another? She wept and sang the praises of her husband; and then, as if to bring her grief to an even higher pitch, the tore the coverings off the litter and exposed the corpse to the night air, weeping and wailing. Falteringly, and knowing how trite and ineffectual his words must sound, Ibrahim tried to tell her that somewhere, even in her great grief, at least a particle of the Mercy of God must be hidden, when suddenly his eyes fell upon the exposed corpse. He gave a great start, and his tongue failed him: The corpse of the husband was wearing the Golden Cloak!

Seeing his astonishment, the widow stopped wailing. 'What has struck you so?' she asked. 'What have you seen?' Trembling, and hardly able to make himself understood, Ibrahim told her the history of the Golden Cloak in which her husband was to be buried; he told her about his encounter with the robbers, his imprisonment in the king's fortress, his rejection by his family, and his years of aimless wandering. And slowly, as he spoke, the widow became calm, and wept no more. When his story was finished, the woman said: 'Hearing this tale of your sorrow has lifted a great burden from my heart; how can my few days of sorrow compare with your years of suffering and exile? I had forgotten that death is but the beginning of a journey; forgive me for my unseemly behavior.' Stammeringly, Ibrahim replied that no forgiveness is required where there is no offense. 'Your story has been like a miracle of Allah,' she said. 'How can I ever repay you? Ah! I know just the thing. Nothing can satisfy me unless you will accept the gift of the Golden Cloak, which is more yours than my husband's. He already carries with him the provisions for his journey, while you, poor homeless wanderer, have nothing and no one in this world.' And so, humbly and with many protests, Ibrahim accepted the Golden Cloak. When dawn broke the next day the funeral procession passed on, and Ibrahim made ready to follow them. But what of the Golden Cloak? How could he wear it now? His years of struggle and suffering had changed the heart in his breast. Yet how could he leave it behind? At last he tied the cloak in a bundle, placed it on his back, and resumed his aimless wandering. But though he was still unsure of his destination, somehow he felt, after his encounter with the widow, that a great burden had been lifted from his heart.

One day in early Spring, when the Sun was bright and the Rain had woven a thin carpet of green over the Earth, Ibrahim, who had been traveling since before dawn, encountered on the road an old man of venerable aspect, wearing a worn and patched cloak. 'Where are you traveling to, my son?' he said, 'and what is in that bundle you carry on your back?' 'Where I am traveling to God only knows, uncle; I am without any path but the one I make with my steps. As for this bundle on my back, it is the famous Golden Cloak.' 'The Golden Cloak,' said the old man; 'that must be worth 10,000 dinars. Tell me, what are you planning to do with it? Are you going to sell it for its value in gold coins?' 'No,' replied Ibrahim. 'Then you must be planning to wear it.' 'No,' replied Ibrahim. 'Ah yes, I see, very wise, undoubtedly you fear to attract robbers; but tell me—what *are* you going to do with it? Are you going to make a gift of it to someone?'

Ibrahim was taken aback by the old man's question, and pondered how to respond. He had done with wearing it, that much was certain. And he had already sold it once, and bought poverty with its price. Why in the name of Allah was he carrying it on his back? What, in fact, was left for him to do but give it away? 'I would rather answer with actions than words, my Master; take it, it is yours.' And Ibrahim removed the bundle from his back, opened it, and handed the old man the Golden Cloak. 'What a wonderful gift,' the old man said, 'and believe me, I have a use for it. But here, you must take something of my own; I cannot allow you to do this thing without expressing my gratitude.' And so saying, the old man removed his worn, patched cloak, and handed it to Ibrahim. Immediately a great change came over him. A great light shone out of him. His beard, that had been white, became black and glossy. The jewels and threads of the Golden Cloak shot rays in all directions, as if touched with the Sun: Thus the old man in the patched cloak was revealed as an angel of God; Ibrahim fell prostrate before him.

'Now you see,' said the angel, 'that this cloak, which you valued so highly, but which proved worthless to you in the markets of the world, does indeed hold all the value you imbued it with, and infinitely more. Your valuation, in fact, was far too low, your paltry degree of admiration insulting to the sublimity of this garment. You valued it only as high as your own vanity, while *it* saw in *you* the Knowledge of Allah. This is why it came into your life, and clung to you like a loyal friend, and always returned to be with you, even through great hardship. But perhaps vanity for knowledge is not, all in all, a bad exchange. Nevertheless, the cloak has now been returned to its rightful owner, because only in this moment has it been given with an open hand, neither stolen, nor bartered, nor sold. There is nothing inside this cloak but knowledge; consequently knowledge may be your companion from now on, and accompany you in all your travels. But as for the tiny particle of knowledge called "The Tale of the Faqir with the Golden Cloak", its time to speak is now ended.'

# THREE POEMS
# OF *AL-QUTB*

## THE SALT OF THE GUIDE

I dove under the disks of the harrow;
I was torn by the blades, became one with
    the field—
And the Farmer who harrowed me
Was HE.
I lay beneath the surface of the water
Holding a hatchet in my right hand and
    another in my left—
And the Stag who stood above me
On the surface of the windy ocean
Was HE.
Hell cures us from Paradise, and Paradise
    from the fires of this world.
Quicksilver for an angry man, says the
    physician's art,
Brimstone for a fool—
But nothing crystallizes, the work is not
    complete
Until the missing ingredient is supplied:
The Salt of the Guide.

UNDER THE HAMMER

When you were at work in the quarry, breaking
    rocks
A willing slave, a king hid in a ruin
I went and lay down
Under the hammers of your remembrance.
What I had made of myself, you unmade
With the craft of the quarryman and the
    mason.
When you were at work in the smithy,
A coal black smith, face gone dark
From staring into the fire,
I went into the forge and lay down
Under the bellows of your remembrance.
Your face gave light
Till I reached white heat. What refuge
    from the hammer, except on the anvil?
What refuge from the fire
But in the forge itself?
What does it matter if I become a cup or
    a blade, a stirrup or an axe-head
If I bear the stamp of the Master?


YA PIR!

Your quality is that of the Autumn Jewel:
Everything is elsewhere, nothing is here;
The world is empty. We are sad because of it.

We are sad because God is lonely for us.
The single, distant star that unfolds
Into the vast plain of Paradise, draws us.

We are lost in this world because of you;
We are in love with the inconceivable
Because we cannot know you as you are.

The sun that sets here, in this empty world
That sinks below the horizon of dust
When evening summons its shadows to
    fill the empty hall

Now rises in the Night of Union.